THE IOWA
ANTHOLOGY
of NEW
AMERICAN
POETRIES

THE IOWA ANTHOLOGY *of* NEW American POETRIES

Edited by REGINALD SHEPHERD

UNIVERSITY *of* IOWA PRESS
IOWA CITY

University of Iowa Press,
Iowa City 52242
Copyright © 2004 by the
University of Iowa Press
All rights reserved
Printed in the United States of America
Design by Richard Hendel
http://www.uiowa.edu/uiowapress

The University of Iowa Press is a member of
Green Press Initiative and is committed to
preserving natural resources.

Printed on acid-free paper

Library of Congress
Cataloging-in-Publication Data
The Iowa anthology of new American
poetries / edited by Reginald Shepherd.
p.   cm.
Includes bibliographical references and
index.
ISBN 0-87745-908-8 (cloth),
ISBN 0-87745-909-6 (pbk.)
1. American poetry—21st century.
I. Shepherd, Reginald, 1963–.
PS617.I55 2004
811'.608—dc22   2004047894

04 05 06 07 08 c 5 4 3 2 1
04 05 06 07 08 p 5 4 3 2 1

For Robert Philen

contents

INTRODUCTION

I

This anthology collects the work of twenty-four poets whose work crosses, ignores, or transcends the variously demarcated lines between traditional lyric and avant-garde practice. Their work combines lyric allure and experimental interrogation toward the production of a new synthesis that I call, after Wittgenstein, lyrical investigations. They are not fence-sitters, but rather are creating and surveying distinctive and extensive territories all their own.

I include both poets who have and poets who have not yet published books; all are writing fully accomplished work. None has published a book before 1990. Severe space constraints have necessitated that I restrict contributors to those who have, at the time of selection, published no more than two full-length books of poetry. As a result, several very talented poets whose work I had originally intended to include, among them Peter Gizzi, Brian Henry, Claudia Keelan, Timothy Liu, Suzanne Paola, and Elizabeth Willis (all of whom have published three or more books), have had to be excluded, on the grounds that their work is less in need of the exposure this anthology may provide than is that of less well published contributors. I urge interested readers to seek out their work.

Though in various stages of emergence into public attention, the contributors to this anthology are not all "younger" poets. Unlike most recent anthologies of new poets, this one is not organized around chronological age. Many such anthologies have been excellent efforts, but the work included has had little sense of commonality other than synchrony. This anthology aims at no such representative sampling. While the directions it points toward are exciting and vital, they are hardly the only valid and interesting territories for contemporary American poetry. However, these directions have rarely been explicitly laid out and brought together.

These are some new American poetries that most fruitfully reach back toward the Modernists and toward earlier lyric poetries (such as those of Wyatt, Donne, Keats, Dickinson, and Hopkins) and simultaneously reach forward to poetic possibilities not yet realized or even imagined. Wallace Stevens noted that all poetry is experimental poetry. Within the constraints mentioned above, I have chosen poets whose experiments most compel me.

II

What I value most in poetry is passion, a passion that manifests itself most immediately in the words which are the poem's body *and* its soul. I find this passionate intensity in the verbal argosies of Hart Crane's "Voyages," in the sly obliquity and exuberant surprise of Dickinson's "I would not paint a picture," or in the chilly intimacies of Stevens's "The Snow Man." The work of all of the poets in this anthology, in various ways, manifests this lyric intensity and passion.

Much contemporary American poetry is embarrassed by passion, by large gestures and major aspirations, as if they were immodest at best, dishonest at worst. As Jorie Graham has said in an interview with critic Thomas Gardner, "we have been handed down by much of the generation after the modernists—by their strictly secular sense of reality (domestic, confessional), as well as by their unquestioned relationship to the act of representation—an almost untenably narrow notion of what [poetry] is capable of." This inheritance still dominates the poetic mainstream, despite the many and diverse openings of the field since then. American poetry still tends to dismiss or ignore those possibilities which cannot be neatly packaged and contained. Among poets who reject the dominant modes, including those who see themselves as experimental or even "oppositional," too many retreat into easy sarcasm and tidy ironies.

But such poets as Kathleen Fraser, Jorie Graham, Ann Lauterbach, Michael Palmer, and Donald Revell have taken up some of the lapsed projects of Modernism, unafraid to confront the larger questions of word and world with which Modernism grappled: as Graham has said in the same interview quoted above, "many poets writing today realize we need to recover a high level of ambition, a rage, if you will—the big hunger." Even in their critiques of Modernism, these poets recognize the possibilities that Modernism offers the contemporary poet, possibilities often foreclosed or simply ignored by both the poetic mainstream and the self-appointed experimental opposition. Michael Palmer has said that though he is sympathetic to and even inspired by much of the work of Language poetry, he is not and could never be a Language poet, because of his commitment to the lyric. A commitment to the lyric means, for one thing, that the self, however problematized and decentered, is not discarded; it also means that beauty is not banished as obsolete or dishonest. Such a commitment rejects a purely negative or critical role for poetry, for art in general (what poet Joshua Corey calls the corrosive postmodern "No," these days too often reduced to an even more corrosive postmodern "Whatever"), in favor of one that, while incorporating critique and interrogation, emphasizes poetry's creative potential, the capacity not only to critique the actually existing world, but to propose alternative possibilities, the other-than of utopia.

Many newer poets, exploring the paths pointed out by the poets mentioned above, as well as by such diverse poets as Michael Anania, Mei-mei Berssenbrugge, Lucie Brock-Broido, Alice Fulton, Allen Grossman, Brenda Hillman, Nathaniel Mackey, Susan Mitchell, John Peck, Bin Ramke, Peter Sacks, Aaron Shurin, Susan Stewart, and Cole Swensen, have unembarrassedly embraced the rhetorical and verbal splendors of the lyric tradition. In her introduction to *The Best American Poetry 1990*, Jorie Graham notes "a renewed fascination with very high diction, surfaces that call attention to themselves" in some recent poetry, while Marjorie Perloff, in introducing a selection of new poets, has commented on an "enormous care for the materiality of words," as well as "a new interest in Beauty, the aesthetic, the pleasure of the text." At the same time such poets remain alert to the seductions of such splendors: they neither stop their ears to the sirens nor are lured onto the rocks by them. They sing, and see, and say, and refuse to choose one over the other.

III

The poets assembled here respect Ezra Pound's injunction to "Make it new," but they don't seek novelty for its own sake, nor do they confuse the merely novel with the new. Remembering that "origin" and "originality" have the same root, these poets also keep in mind Pound's observation that "What thou lovest well remains." What they love is the singing line of the lyric tradition, however broken the song may be.

These are all poets who, whatever their interrogations of language and discourse, still cherish the enchantments of the lyric, poets who leap the chasms between what the brilliant critic Charles Altieri calls lyricism and lucidity. T. S. Eliot wrote that the poet must be as intelligent as possible, while Wallace Stevens wrote that the poem must resist the intelligence almost successfully.

Following in this line, these poets reject the dichotomy of thought and emotion, feeling thoughts and thinking feelings in the way that Eliot said the metaphysical poets did. They problematize the self without rejecting its affective possibilities, and neither reify feeling nor undercut it with reflexive and evasive irony—they don't fear emotion, but they don't fetishize it either. They accept the inevitability and the creative opportunities of fracture without embracing fragmentation for its own sake or for the sake of a statement about contemporary life. Conversely, they eschew unselfconscious narrative without abandoning the pleasures and possibilities of story, however oblique, indirect, and/or incomplete.

These poets explore some of the myriad potentials of the word as such while still holding fast to the protean demon of content, grappling fiercely with its ballasts and its resistances. For these poets, artifice refines and intensifies passion, and passion checks and channels artifice—their poems are deeply felt *and* deeply formed. Their poetry matters and has matter.

These poets fulfill the terms of what Allen Grossman has called the four tasks that the significant poet must be expected to perform: to point out what is significant in the world of common experience; to defeat given expectations with respect to how things are assembled (and poems themselves are very much in the category of "things"); to make clear how difficult it is to make meaning; and to make clear how interesting the world is. They are restless and searching, unafraid to be radical and ambitious in their engagements with both word and world. They don't accept easy answers (including the easy answers of negation), but they refuse to dismiss the possibility of answers. While understanding that creation often entails critique, they are charting new territories of lyrical exploration, producing new possibilities for poetry and for our lives.

These poets do not disdain communication, but they know that communication is as difficult and complex as it is urgent and necessary: they understand intellectually and viscerally the need to break through the crusts of habit and routine, of the already-said that says nothing over and over. They are all poets for whom the self is neither cynosure nor mystification, but rather an open question, something to be constructed (or construed), poets for whom experience is not prior to the poem but something we undergo with and within the poem, for whom the poem itself is an experience.

For all of them, as for Mallarmé, poems are made out of words, not out of ideas or emotions, though their poems certainly enact and embody emotions and ideas: they also question and even erase the distinction between these two realms. As I wrote above, these poets have passion—their poems are not cold, though in some the fires may be banked, thus burning more intensely—yet their hearts are not on their sleeves but in their words. These are poets who, in the German critical theorist Theodor Adorno's words, alienate language from its alienation in use, bringing the word back to itself, bringing us as readers back to ourselves. They do not disdain or dismiss beauty, though they know that all true beauty has some proportion of strangeness and that, as H. D. insisted, beauty must have strength, and they will not settle for the easy and easily repeated beauties of the already-known. Finally but not last, and recalling lyric's origins in the lyre, none of them forgets to bring the music.

I'd like to thank Brian Henry and Kevin Prufer for generously sharing their editorial experience and acumen, and for introducing me to the work of several wonderful writers. I'd also like to thank Peter Gizzi and Timothy Liu for their advice and suggestions. I thank Robert Philen for his constant love, support, and encouragement as I worked on this project.

Dan Beachy-Quick

Artist's Statement

and had you the leisure to tell me

A *poetic*, if true, exists as does Heraclitus's river—it is never the same twice. There is no authority, even with the author, to say more than: "Here. Here is where I've stepped in now—now in this current." As the water eddies around the ankle, so another current eddies around the poem: the lyric takes shape in such whirlpools created in trespass, in entrance, and in motion. Step out. The surface heals by the very motion that created the wound—it is new, the water, and it carries down stream a history of who entered it and when. This is a living history. Such is Tradition: alive.

Such thinking unfolds itself in the letter Thomas Higginson pulled from the envelope sent by Emily Dickinson. First sentence: "Are you too deeply occupied to say if my verse is alive?" And later: "Should you think it breathed—and had you the leisure to tell me, I should feel quick gratitude." *Quick*, here, describes not rapidity, but the root of the word: life and blood. A poetic in the vein. The living poem speaks to the living; and Tradition (those poems whose thinking has existed through these centuries) is not to be imagined as the museum's walls through which we in half-wonder walk, but rather is the throat pulsing, is the wrist pulsing, is the aortic arch. The poem, I think, we find, as Empedocles writes: "nurtured in the seas of rebounding blood, where most especially is what is called thought by humans, for the blood round the human heart is thought." Mine, I hope, is a quick blood: my poetic pulsing in my name.

The confusion between heart and mind is, to some degree, equivalent to Keats's *negative capability*. Yes, it denies an "irritable reaching after fact and reason." But more, it offers the radical assumption that form does not simply exist as form, but rather, the poet's mind pulses, the poet's heart thinks. Form is dashed line, not solid boundary. If we put on a mask in a dramatic monologue, we do so not for the mask's sake, but for the voice spoken through another's mouth that is also our own.

I mean to give a *poetic*—I mean to do so lovingly. And so, I find my thoughts become others' thoughts. Not mine. I express them as my own; for the length of this page, or the length of my life, perhaps they are. A living poetic, a loving poetic, is one which understands how each poem, how each form, is but one instant of a vaster current, and never is complete in itself. I mean no easy gesture toward the fragment, the lacunae, toward rupture. I mean simply this: a poem written in love risks absence, risks being incomplete, privileges the unknown over what's at hand—the poem betrothed to revealing the world in which it lives.

I work at The School of the Art Institute of Chicago. Working at a museum gives me an intimacy with its art that is hard to describe except by tracing for you the galleries in which I find myself walking. Past Redon's flowers turning into butterflies, past Schwitters's *merz* collages, past the collection of mast-heads from Puritan America (the women staring off into the ocean that is not there, clutching to their breasts a bible, a book), I find myself most often wandering through Tang Dynasty funerary pieces. Many are broken. The glazes—almost garish greens, a mustard yellow—meld into one another (the process not yet mastered). And some in particular catch my attention. The protective spirits holding wooden spears—only the wood has eroded away. When I walk down the steps, I have this image in my mind—I don't even know if the piece exists. A flautist playing music in the grave. Except, the flute carved of wood is gone. He holds to his mouth the absence of the flute to play the flute's music. Such is my poetic, now. To put his flute to my lips and play this tune (mine and not mine)—the instrument of air being the only one suited to making music out of breath.

Then Dickinson, again: Should you think it breathed—

Echo & A

Speak into water,   a
Name bent at the knee.
Speak close to.
Does the surface bend
Back at breath,   am

I that loudly
Yours? Knee bent on some
Name. Your eye half-closed. That river
White at noon is blank
At eclipse. An iris, a crown—speak

Curve into dark water,   does
The surface darken
Back at breath,   am I
That loud in you, bent on knee
To speak water bright

On bright wave? A sun in edges
Ripples to shore. A day
In lines, under water, an hour
Shores in a year. Open
Your eye and the lake is open,

Knee bent at a name. Narrow
Your eye and the lake
Thins, gains speed at squint—
Behind lids,   an
Aquifer below the arroyo

Of your closed eye,   and me
Kneeling on a name.
I wouldn't speak that day.
At the lake edge, remember
The minnows

On unseen fins turn on shadows
To quicken the eye
Closed. Before: each silver
Fish its own light flamed under
Water, speak it,   a

Constellation beneath waves.
Those shadows
Were ours that snuffed that
Cosmos out
By nearing it. That darkness

Tangent to the severed wing
Of the moth—
At each wave the dead wing fluttered
And seemed to fly—
That darkness was the sun

Behind me, behind my head, speaking
A name. The moth wing
In flight inside me
Under water, to touch my
Tongue to water

I bent my knees to speak.
The sun in waves beneath us
Speaks: *wife, wish, hush, wife.*
I lake to calm. You river
To leave. Sun in eclipse,   a

Pupil, an iris, a crown
Curve, water curves the bank
Of the lake the lake's lips—
O, darkly   narrow
                    and then
O, filled with light.

Halt (Naïve)

(in which I see our condition is as Ishmael's, who says: "Ahab's quenchless feud seemed mine." We examine the qualities of the White Whale to understand that feud—No, I mean, the quenchlessness)

A. MOBY DICK

Theory of Pursuit: there is no me minus you
And you I cannot prove. Ask the equation

Where that leaves me, afloat, afloat, a
Wooden Hull on waters I charted

But I do not know. You-at-depths I know—
And I know you-surfacing. You made of me

One syllable, a single-point, and at my touch
(Whale) you multiplied wave by wave until ocean

Bore no nearing you, except by halving distance
The wind in sail already halved. Zeno says:

None touch. I have touched and been touched both.
A single-point, I see you are everywhere.

Sailors swear to your breaching in two
Opposite latitudes at once. You fold

Circumference into center—you tell me both
Are one. True, I witness, I attest. A ghost-nerve

Electric in the ghost-leg aches. My captain's
Leg lurks in you still, and you lurk everywhere.

B. MOBY DICK

Mute latitudes, blind: the ocean mutters dumb
The jellyfish's phosphorescent thumb (stinger),

Mutters dumb the dark ink inside the squid
That is the White Whale's food. The ocean stings

The bit lip shut: *I misspoke, I see I misspoke.*
The ocean mutters: "no more, no more" (a message

Spoke not only to shore). I hear what I am told.
No ears are deaf save those that need not hear:

Who below the ocean knows the ocean
Murmurs most darkly to itself. White Whale—

Sailing-men say you do not die, you do not die—
You in silence, silent lie, and flame your thought

Toward what uncharted depth-of-mind you'll divine:
Chapter Closed. Me? Coral reef? Captain

Or a Captain's leg? A flaming-thought thinks
Itself, you do, you do. Your silent white, the dark shark

Flees from in fright. No tooth threatens you,
You know. You know

Men think your silent tongue is dumb and mute with nacre—
I suspect—your dumb tongue is dumb—as is a sodden acre.

C. MOBY DICK

A prophet is a man with a river-bed
For a face, and no water.

Reeds bend in wind to speak, and he tells them:
No. Breathe dust. He is dust speaking

To dust. A prophet does not speak
For himself. *Who?* A river

Empty bleeds into ocean full. Go to ocean.
Put my hand beneath water, and my hand

Is held by what it cannot hold, belongs
To wave's cresting arm, to the wrist

Whose pulse is the ripple back from shore:
I learn so to make myself not my own.

The White Whale below water holds his breath—
He is breath by water held. As I am dust

Stitched into skin, a whale is water thickened
Into skin, depth unknown. A god

Erases himself to make himself known. At fathoms
Whale, at fathoms, I'm the bent reed beside you

Asking you . . . as men on ocean do . . . asking you
Why fill your lungs at latitudes no man knows?

Why must I next to you be but a speaking mote?
Not true, not true. I'm a river-bed. I've tried

To imagine in you a silt-layer of words you
Will not speak. Will you, Dumb God?

No river flows to you to answer for you
Your "No."

D. MOBY DICK

No reverie begs "light" in the blind eye.
Reverie says: dig this *depth-of-blank*

Deeper (mute-God, blind-God). Dig deeper
With the Whale below the white-capped waves—

A twitch of his tail, a twitch of his white tail
Birthed from ocean-bed the wave

That broke calm water into each cracked plank
Of the harpooner's boat, made that man sway,

And cast him on the spear his arm meant to sling
At you. Beneath the sun's evil weight

Men burn nightwards but never darken
Past night. There's always the moon's hook

On still water to deny them their eyes'
Closing. But Whale, you dive down

Until the ocean's ground begs you solid, "Stop."
Whale, White Whale, you do not stop.

You beat your head against the jagged rocks.
Blind in depths so dark light itself is blind,

You knock your head against the rocks to see
And scratch the god-itch from your thoughts.

Flame is jealous of flame, once lit, and ever
Reaches higher. You wait, match-tip, Whale,

I see how you wait in silence for silence
To say: *write it in, tell me who I am now.*

Nightbook

A decade and the small world in chrysalis
Hatches from hunger to hungerless wings
Hungerless flight   yes, *saturnid*   yes, *sulfur*
(Or, from the nest at night)   yes, *passerine*

Horizon betrothed to horizon rings the whole
World's arching circumference the same curve
As of your curving eye, and both will blink
Shut, both will blind, will be blind—

Here on midnight waters, some stars still burn,
Some still burn, devoted to the blank
Surface they mar. Pray quiet but cannot be

Quiet as rose
Petal of quartz in stone. No finger in the ore-deep dawn
No dawn   No down at wingtip   No dawn
Save the furthest star on this water glowing

A clear devotion   speaks to us this clearly
Love not principle   Love not geometric

All night the heavenly angles sing loose
Their acute labor, Orion's arrow at a sparrow shot,
The north star longing to betray north, the moon
Veiled from *luna*, hidden from moths, this world

This chaos in my mouth I love you
With such shadow, such silence
                                        wife
Put out those stars
Wet wing against the water brushing

Botany

My orchid-me had need to keep in thrall
The wasp. I thought: *You were*. My mimic
Blank-petal unfurling low, I thought
Your dark abdomen: *mine*   was mine.

Did not think me. My own, I wanted
You to think: *You were*. Not you
On nerved wings, my sepal petals
Mimic me   you.

You above my hovering. I hover.
A fast wing seems not. To move
Wasp, I
Gain speed to keep me still. You

Sting air to hang motionless. In air
You stun I stem me. Not to look
You don't look. You don't
Bite the pinched stem to   fall down.

I hold me open. In ways you do not
Know. Me, wasp? Master, yourself? Whose
Empty mouth swallows the mouth
More empty. Ask me. My name I named you

(Master, I) named you Stingless (Master
Who's) named you
Stamen when (mastering whom?) you sting
I orchid me, I buzz. You sepal, Wasp you. Unfold.

Flag-Tree

Heard in air those words I later made me read—
Cut, by a leaf, in two. (Be plainer, still.)

A leaf cut-in-two taught the air to read.
Air begged, *Be my tongue.* When the leaf stood still,

It refused. (Be plain. Still.) I know the tree
I speak of: doubled-over-in-wind. Wind

Tangled no ribbon in the branch-tangled tree.
No knot-of-hair (your hair) branch-knotted, by wind.

A flag-tree grows where wind blows most: *furious.*
When wind dies, the tree seems not-to-know—

Bends down, still blown. "What does this mean—for us?"
You said (not there). I don't know. (Be plain.) I know

The leaf says, *Wind*—must, as wind through it blows.
Ask me again—how you asked me how—to tell me: *No.*

Stellar Elements

Rewind the star back to a burning rind—
Un-collapse that flame. Flame fused, refused

Its molten thought—*iron*—that is its mind
's undoing. See how the cast-out thought cooled

Into diamond? Light slows down into stone.
Stone thinks: *nothing*. A stone, hand-held, becomes the hand

's dense thinking: *profit me more*. To own
The ore, dismiss the rock to flame. Flame demands:

My furnace. Furnace wants me to: *un-earth*
One pound—more—of coal. Dark thought remains

Inside the tree: *the axe cannot breathe*
As I can breathe. Axe, colder than flame—

Does flame's job. Cuts to that stone inside the wood—
Dull stone whose ore is how the star was caught.

Jasper Bernes

Artist's Statement

I am less and less interested, poetry-wise, in the facts and contingencies of my own life, although the awareness of having a life certainly impinges upon the poems as I write them. This constitutes a grudging and partial acceptance of Eliot's aesthetic in "Tradition and the Individual Talent." And if, on the other side of the veil, I find myself attracted to a particularly interesting formation of cumulus clouds, the plans for the World Trade Center site, a tree or bird that swims into my dingy windows, or the elusive Higgs Boson, these are less material for poems than they are the source of new imaginative lexicons. Perhaps I am uncomfortable or nauseated with having a life in the era of the multinational corporation and the War on Terror; perhaps my poems are too.

"In the presence of the violent reality of war," writes Wallace Stevens, "consciousness takes the place of the imagination. And consciousness of an immense war is a consciousness of fact." He distinguishes this narrowing down to the actual from his own poetry of the imagination, which "illustrates the fundamental and endless struggle with fact." Stevens suggests that to write imaginative poems, to write away from the world-historical, agitates courageously against "the desire to move in the direction of fact as we want it to be." If so, then these days a poetry of the imagination degreases the wheels of the fact-producing and fact-corroborating war-machine.

My manuscript, *Interference*, from which some of these poems originate, would engage in such imaginative acts of interference, inference, and collided reference. The poems in this collection, however, risk grandiosity and magical thinking; the speaker of the poems indulgently sees himself as inextricably complicit in the violence of history. Imagination, in many of these poems, gives way to fact; irony and comedy fail the speaker as useful tools with which to articulate his own responsibility or lack thereof. Things get confused. The "struggle with fact" in these poems fails, I would hope instructively, precisely because they seem to refer to a real life, a personal experience, that everywhere bottlenecks their performances. I am too interested, in these poems, in the human. In my more recent poems, I have sought to limit the influence of my own life. I have sought a writing where the poem produces its author and audience, rather than the other way around; where meanings are provisional, the by- and waste-products of a thought in motion, rather than ends in and of themselves. I now prefer, where possible, performative language to descriptive language, meditation to narrative, texture to detail, precision to accuracy, multiplicity's embarrassment of riches to singularity's stark finitude, insides to outsides. Whether I have succeeded here I cannot judge; nonetheless, these be my aims.

I take as my hero and mascot the cartoon character who draws and erases and redraws the room in which he resides, the frazzled coyote whose bag of tricks is as endless as his mark is elusive. Perhaps such a frame is in fact a prison, but it is one whose endless and bottomless interiors exhilarate. And although this kind of poetry might make nothing happen, for Stevens such nothing is as positive as it is negative. It is not easy to make nothing *happen*; especially in a world where *everything* might, and where, for most of the time, I'm but a blip on the actuarial tables of Stevens's beloved Hartford Life.

Sonnet with Lock and Key

Build it here.
     Where the drenched vespers quarry air,
where here is far.
     Build, of flower-
split rock and wasp-scored
marble, summers in a marmalade of shiver.

Let the names contain their names and nothing more.
Let light inflate its splendors to
the pressure of the gentlest touch
rebuffed.
    Let it candelabra upward
or chandelier down into the dear
marrow-sense of error everywhere at odds
with other terror. Awe's the law here
and what's left (of what's left).
          You come with your
mouth bunched in your hands, with your knees
like stray fire, and you stay, you sleep
in the shape of a key you cannot quite wield.

Found Missing

Write the last rules first: that each specific
lists, infinitely, what it is not. Beneath
a foot of snow the squirrel-gray child's glove
(with its worn squirrel insignia) in place of
a glove-gray (dead) baby squirrel, in place
of the child himself, lost, as he had wished,
in place of the glove: not finding one morning
a new pair of gloves but a man's unmanacled
hands, a hidden flight of stairs behind
the refrigerator, behind the frigid air,
where lives a house unlike the dead one he's
made his fault—because he cannot unfasten
his hand from his hand, because he is what happened
happening again, loss that can't once found be lost.
I don't blame him or begrudge his box of broken
toys, his name games whose rules are
eliminated, one by one, with each move;
his failings confected from mismatched sets.
Even in winter he asks when we'll play Frisbee
and I lie, and he lies back best he can.
Around us the town has built a new library, while
slouched asleep in a chair the woman I give
my empties to, with a picture book of Morocco. . . .
He can read now, which complicates things: one
Election Day I watched his friends and him take
turns lying in the outline chalked on the sidewalk.
Weren't like anything, he says, when I ask: one
glove worse than none, such orphanages where
the pairless complements are sent, the unborn
brothers born of divorced or dead fathers, non-
existent antonyms misused out of the dictionary.
Eight dollars and yet the mortmain of each exclusive
snowflaked fact tamps the involuted edges down
into downy metonymic abysses. I'm not thinking of him.
I'm from all combos writing one messy little sentence
about someone else I know by what she's not
and only that, not sullen or sunny, not fey
or extravagant, how in her absence
the absence of these attributes fits, but not like a

as I've said—any love I could wear.

Rave

Ravel of ravishments   the raven-black
interstices   of the cat-walked
factory-guts.   Below which the revelers
their engines   *rêve*
overheating   the revelers orchidized
with chemical, chimerical crystals of x.

It is a scene, Act X.
                A small door
opens high in the mind: two girls
with daisy-stickers on their nipples
slip into the mix, while
                phased lights agitate and valve
the crowd, as toward an epilepsy or cure.
The DJ puts the song into reverse, lets it out
then backs again. No one belongs to their bodies as to a paternalistic order
                anymore;
balloons of anaesthetic gas pass hand to hand and when
the mind returns it finds itself inside
another's numbed, Apollonian torso.

One of the ones one was wanders
all night in this way, *ill-assorted, contra-*
                dictory.
Looking for his legs. A whisper craven in the dregs. Except

it is The Earth here too. Overburdened with product, with invention.
Restorative in its seasonal self-destructions, tectonic musics

Clang and Rattle, Bang, Shake, Rock and Roll

And although we have learned to live inside our bodies without irony
                or completion
when from miles within the unearned earth   we could have loved you
high heaved over us   waves of breaking glass   a force catches fire
and which seems   in falling frames   to just hang there   arresting you.

Desiderata on a Desert Island

Each island marks the limits of the sight,
Each prisoner the center of a prism, thousand-
Faced, wherein the vision of the others

Drowns in confounded distances. This
Is our city, our archipelago of sprawl,
On self-love built: one long block out, as on

A ring of reef, the repeated, bleeding gazes
Founder and collapse, sun-bald, like waves
Under the overambitious topweight of a forward push.

The horizon is a second skin, seeing
Sheathed by being, swallowed whole.
It kings us eye for I. It brings what

Flings us far near, a myopia, a fat
Cataract where the ocean pours over
The edge into threshing, blent serrations, scales.

Retinal flotsam, rods and cones,
Wash ashore—eyechart letters, blurs
That form no common language. We must

Build then with lack a private
Shack, a charm for the sharks, a diction
Wholly homegrown. We were allowed to bring

One word each. We were allowed to choose.
My sister, protectless now, and lost, picked
Justice. I hear her hear here, sometimes, in the waves

Just this, just this, the beach each day
Leveled in the steady bevel of the tides,
Its hall of mirrors. An old friend, in front of us

At the all-night processing center,
Whispered *verdant* to the guards. She must
Live then with, for scenery, the names of trees and flowers

She's never seen, garden overgrown with unknowing.
Impossible to gauge the time it's taken
To pen these notes, with only the empty

Amphitheater of the ocean, with only subtle
Inflections to distinguish one thought
From another, blue from green, gulls from pelicans,

Where exactly and how the water becomes
symbol of a common, consanguineous solitude.
Is that love? God? Justice? What I feel

Seems to name the others farther and more pure.
Inarticulable difference, loves without object.
Sometimes the palm, grown so familiar, so commonplace,

Disappears in the empty-scented tradewinds,
Winnowed by excessive adoration.
My glyph's *desiderata*, a stiff wind or wand of wishes

Which no longer refer to any world I can recall.
In name alone. A hive, a latin hum
Of what's not here and never was.

And in this way Los Angeles is made.

South Central Notes toward a Shooting Script

The camera is cousin of the gun, as
harnessed violence, stolen quasar fire,
burns behind the burnished buttons of undress.

She hits the button marked "withdrawal."

In the confusion caused by "to shoot."
Gasoline, torn t-shirt, beer bottle.
The fires in infrared from the helicopters
a map perhaps of anomie or scrounge.

Sorry but we are unable to process your
request at this time.

Skyscrapers swoon. *Delirium tremens* of recession.
Co-co Ri-co Chicken, flame broiled.
Oppress the buttons. Agencia de Viajes.

A paradigmatic dissolve—greened to blue the eerily-
marine, Cerberal or cerebrally-serrated tongues of flame
pile at the edges of a purl of junk bonds.
A TV in a broken, ovening storefront; a TV in a living room.
The bass line from "Burning and Looting," hacking cough of helicopter

Stand back. Stand back. We regret
to inform you that the Los Angeles
Police Department has declared moral
and intellectual bankruptcy. I'll kill you, bitch.

~~Christopher Columbus Transcontinental~~ Highway.
American Indian. Martin Rodney Luther
King Jr. Boulevard.

To wit. At one of apostasy's
metastasizing, slipped epicenters.
Quiver of police tape. Do not cross.
Stretched taut between *seeing* and *doing*.

If you point a video camera at its output
source you'll see God. The jaws of life.

To wit. Circuit City: Electronics Appliances
Car Home. Switch to black-and-white.

Fast stock. Wide angle. A wading feel.
A slow motion quicksand-of-the-moment feel.

Three black women, one in pink pumps,
pitched forward at a half run across
the debris-strewn parking lot. One films
with a stolen camera. The third waves.

Reverse shot: three white adolescents
also filming from a stopped car. Them filming them filming them.
And on and on. It breaks the plane. And the gaze
skips, the gaze bounces
back and forth, no stable point-of-view.
Little infinity. Little chiasmus.

The women get in their black Mercedes and drive away.
They didn't need the camera. But we love them nonetheless.

Outside You Cannot Breathe

Bait for the stricken, stale, red-checked eye,
these placid, flashy fish describe, without parole,
the same unbeginning figure-eight. Trees
scud on the glass; buildings, their windows likewise
scummed with sunset (as if inside were fire)
dissolve to sham sea-forests, miniature shipwrecks
beside which a Santa Claus plants, in mossy pebbles,
an American flag. It wags like a dog's tail, indolent
as the fish who forget, every three seconds, where they've been,
spared thereby what could be called (like hell) a satellite of itself.
Christmas has been cancelled, kids, and these recursive
prisoners remind, without remembering, without not
butting their pouted mouths against the doubled watcher's
watery half-inward gaze, of just that, dead mid-thought.
Hostage to an arrested attempt at self-discovery
but missing by whole measures the errant leisure
such delayed arrival might deliver, repeatedly, like an insult
to the brain, they circle inside us who also eat
our own refuse in a möbius-noose of non-achievement.
Too many fatted vapidities packed into the body's
fifty-gallon vat, like death-in-life, like what a laughable
idea about death life is. Fish brain swimming inside
the larger, wastefully-spacious human brain,
bent in every direction back in on itself, a failed
escape artist, wriggling outward into further fetters—
for our first act, we use the word *malapropism* in-
appropriately, because *there is no outside; outside
you cannot breathe.* We talked, my friend and I,
about last night last night, trying to unsay what
kept getting said just as fast. Tragic to truly think
that all thought to be thought must obsess its own
unsound and groundless prepossessions. We are
repeating ourselves, we said again, and so we were.

CYNTHIA CRUZ

ARTIST'S STATEMENT

Regarding why I write or why I write how I write, all I can say is this: I grew up tending a garden of secrets. A lifetime of secrets, secrets unsaid for generations. I was born in Germany, the daughter of a German woman whose mother walked to daily dance classes during the bombing of Berlin. What she saw (rubble and the dead), and what she knew (the genocide that was happening in her name), remained intact in a small box in her mind. It was there, in my grandmother's mind, that a secret was born. That jewel was passed down to her daughter then down to me. What is not said remains volatile. A land mine waiting to explode. My father is Mexican American; a field worker as a boy. His family came from Chihuahua, a town of revolutionaries. And so I am half silence, half revolutionary. I grew up poor in California, the first of my family to attend college. It would be impossible for me not to attempt to say. And so I became a poet. And so my poetry is fused with sorrow.

In my writing, I mine the same trash heap (history & memory) over and over.

As the French philosopher Helene Cixous writes, "The true secret causes the most suffering, because it is the exact figure of death. If we have a secret we don't tell then we truly are a tomb." I write broken lyrics; shattered glass in the written form. I use metaphor, extended metaphor, music, line break (enjambed or line-broken), persona, and allusions. I collage, at times, song lyrics, historical and biblical writings. I try to project the world onto me: my self as the mirror or Ophelia's pool of water. The sorrows of the twenty-first century sing from the "I" of my poems. But broken, away from the original context, into the lyric form. Not surprisingly, my writing life and my living, breathing, riding the subway life are separated, if at all, by a mere bare thread. Poets whose work has influenced me include Dickinson, Milosz, Edwin Muir, Mahmoud Darwish, Zagajewski, Youssef. Also, of course, James Wright,

Yeats, Berryman, Plath, Shakespeare, Thomas James, and Frank Stanford. The hope is to marry the "terrible" with beauty.

And it is necessary I remain the outsider. For it is only by standing outside the gathering crowd that I can begin to see with a clear eye. To this end, I spend most my time alone, watching the World. I spend hours each day keeping up with news of the World. Literally, the wars, famine, poverty, genocide. A mad scientist, I am trying to find out why.

Impossible as it is, I hope to hold the silver sliver of truth close at all times. It is, I believe, in the unbearable that I find that which one dare not say. What Helene Cixous calls "The School of the Dead," the underworld, where we must not go, we must go. By writing down the unbearable truth, I reconstruct the past. Give memory a house. I have found, as a young writer in the twenty-first century, many of my contemporaries write as if in a void; as if there were no history, no tragedy, no risk involved in telling. I wish to follow in the steps of those who swam up against inertia. Dostoyevsky, Celan, Trakl, Rilke, and W. G. Sebald. I do not live in a vacuum. As I write this in my quiet Manhattan apartment, bombs are being dropped in Baghdad by my government. Why am I not the woman whose home is being destroyed? The woman left to collect her child's bones? Only by God's wrong count am I not. And though I do not claim to write "political poetry," I do hope to write poetry that troubles the reader, for I am troubled by the world I live in.

But, how shall I say the unsayable? As Emily D. said, Tell it slant. And so I go back to the how and why of my writing. I do not live in a vacuum, I am not apart from the suffering of the world. This suffering finds its way into me, thus into my writing. And so my poems are often sad, elegiac, songs. I would like to walk through the world naming. And so I write poems to name, to reconstruct the awful. For it is in the awful that the most beautiful moment arises. With a gun to my head, then the executioner sets the gun down. Freedom is realized as never before. That moment of freedom, that tiny song, is the song I hope to translate into my work. That is my goal. I can't claim to accomplish such a feat, but I can move toward that aim.

Persephone

Mother moves through the World
With her torch of horse hoof and blood-string.
Meanwhile, underneath, bodies are beginning
To fill with tar. Hosts float into the blinding station.
In the dark, beneath the World, we are.
Sleep is a black stain, seeping through.
In my winter dreams,
I crawl out of another girl's history.

Persephone II

A slit in the earth.
I dropped crushed daisies and cornflower
For her to find me.
But the slit healed shut.

The dream keeps repeating: my lost mother
Caught in the Black Garden,
A crown of bees
Spitting circles around her temples.

A blue-orange bee stings my ear.
Now the World is audible.
I hear the earth's skin ripple
As the wind blows through
And thistles clicking like bells.

I did not eat
For seven weeks.
But the fruit looked like a heart
Bleeding beneath the earth.

Seven red seeds
Stitched in the wound of a pomegranate.
Seven red seeds glowing hot like stars.
Something whispered to me. I ate all seven.
Now I am the pulse beneath the earth.

The sky is flooding the trees.
I am trying but I cannot

Drag the river up from the bank.
And my soul is slipping between my fingers.

Listen, there is no God—
Just that chalk-star
Clicking on and off.

Dots of crows march the cornfield.

How to Catch a Ghost in a Jar

That was the summer the bleeding stopped,
The summer the cold took over.
My hands, brittle as bismuth, blind as lab mice.
That was the summer I set the field on fire.
I am a closet of secrets, dying.
In gowns of torn cotton, bits of discarded trash-
Weed, dragged hem, white lace stained black,
I went missing beneath the din of the city.

The door to the World keeps opening and closing.

Briar Rose Waltz

Suitors lined up like sailors
And me, steadying for the Kick.

I've potions flown in from the Deep South;
Trinkets of bruised black tin.

After twenty and some years of woolen-blue sleep,
In a chartreuse gown of hand-sewn lace,

I'll beckon the boys
With a dulcet lilt.

Me, this bare slip
Of a girl.

In the final flash of summer
I'll be thinner and loved

Like no one. At dawn,
I'll dance the last

Lost Bavarian Waltz,
Winged fox that I am.

At the end of the night,
A warm mouth on mine,

I'll be gentled with tender
Hands soaked in brine.

My temples wet with the tongues
Of young gods,

Drunk on the sweet
Sonata of a promise.

Against my damp skin,
Each boy's voice, whispering,

Bleed your wonder, young daughter,
Upon the soft horns of my head.

Traveling Gospel

His hands were moving like twin engines
But his lips unzipped my pants.
He told me, with a voice of cold pennies,
You're the prettiest boy I've ever seen.
In a wasted field of spirit-weed, a few miles
Off the Interstate, a lost trucker gentled me with his slow song
Of longing. And a beautiful orchestra took over
The milk in my veins. A wild sky of semis
Like silver jets taking off—

Self Portrait in Froehlichia

I was out with lanterns
When you arrived with a torch in the night.

In evening weather, I resisted.

In the evening water, I rested
A diadem of cotton
Upon the wet crown of your head.

A locket of Oklahoma summer and the blonde
Leather back-seat of a stolen '68
Studebaker.

Outside the broken window,
A nodding field of rocket and a shot–
Gun of starlings, scattering.

After you vanished,
I waited for the heat to prevail.
Then I prayed.

I wish to be unhinged of all systems.
I want flocks of low flying swan, brutal windstorm, feathered
Lamps by the thousand, dirt
In the hand. And you,

My little winter, I do
Not believe I ever
Imagined you might leave, and

I shall never wish

To see another spring time, ever.

Ariadne, waiting

This is how I was found.

Foxed under in nothing, strewn bare in cinquefoil,
Torn loose of the earth, chanting,
The thought of your body breaks me.
Disquieted child, I fall under spells.
Soon, I will receive you, lie with you,
Mend your salt-stung hands.
When the ocean, envious of your leaving,
Moans to the boats and anchors,
We will dream the coming armada,
A covey of dark birds, the deep asunder—

Praying

I was kneeling in the willow when
The sun fell back into its crib of poison.
The splinter floated before my eyes, again.

I washed my silver handgun and I
Set the last dangerous dream afloat.

The ripped yellow curtains were humming along the sill
As I entered the terrible flowering.

There isn't anything you or anyone can say.
I am my father's only son.

Came evening, like a broken girl limping into the orchard.

Praying

Into the ice ravaged rag-weed and phlox
I vanished.

Goodbye to the Ever-
Blonde Empire,

Its feather gowns and endless
Blue lanterns.

When I reached the jeweled nettle,
I abandoned what little was left
And entered the silence in the Orchard.

I have had a Terror I could tell
To no one.

Praying

When I was set in that field
Like a seed left out for God,
It was like being underwater.
The night, swimming with willow and strange
Beautiful birds. The shadows of
That pasture still rise me from my sleep.
There's a machine-gun silence
Inside me from that field.
Or from someplace else, I don't know.
I hear the girl laughing on the ocean and I think
Of the children I will never have.

Praying

In the middle of the night
Father brought me a falcon.

By morning, it ripped the wire
And flew the hill into the highway.

When they found me
In that car, my sleeve stemmed in blood,
I didn't know what it was
I was trying to kill.

I saw a craft of orphans coming down the river.
They were dressed in white and silent as a séance.

It was then I spoke to the bird.

Already God is shaking his black seed
Back into me.

Jocelyn Emerson

Artist's Statement

In poetry I am compelled by the gaps (linguistic and historical) between words, ideas, feelings, and material reality, i.e., the "negative" spaces that shape thought and emotion, and in which they are shaped at the individual and cultural levels—much as I am compelled by negative theology. I am fascinated by the process of trying to map governing epistemes of putatively antithetical discourses against one another (the "scientific" and the "aesthetic" for example) to see where their mutually exclusive definitions of self and other become visible and audible, without resorting to a default Hegelian dialectic or implicit binary opposition about which Derrida has long since informed us.

It's that moment in which a poem begins for me—in disequilibrium, between the rock and the hard place. Unlike Eliot, I find crises in representation, in metanarratives, to be capacious opportunities—perhaps inherently elegiac, often terrifying, yes—but profoundly generative in the way that natural phenomena are. Such "crises" are also where an ideal poem ends for me. The poetic text both begins and ends *in medias res*, which may or may not be thought of as "indeterminacy." It may happen in free verse or in inherited verse forms, which is why institutional and cultural disagreements about "free verse" and "formal poetry" seem beside the point, not to mention weakly defined in too many cases.

Poems are, for me, almost entirely creatures of their shifting and malleable textual and material histories, rather than chips off the old transcendent block. Enlightenment tropes of mastery, domination, and autonomy don't interest me very much as ways of approaching the writing or reading processes; however, I do find that legacy relevant when considering local issues of linguistic or imagistic precision (i.e., in New Critical method as a late descendant of Kantian aesthetics). This isn't to say that I idealize poems as perishable, but that I would hope that all poems, including my own, have an interesting life apart from their authors within the flux of a much larger cultural poetics, in Stephen Greenblatt's famous term. But that also means they can disappear.

With regard to "the voice," I am extremely wary of its quasi-metaphysical status in contemporary creative writing pedagogy and discourse; it seems to me to be an impossibly reductive and vague term, sentimental. I am also suspicious of essentialist constructions of the body, no matter how progressive the politics of such an impulse may be, as in some formulations of *l'écriture féminine,* for example.

I much prefer active disequilibrium. I admire poets who create poems as inherently liminal texts on the threshold between stability and instability (textual and epistemological) such as Dickinson's "variants" in her fascicles and Stephanie Strickland's hypertexts. Such liminality is perhaps why I find the early modern period endlessly fascinating—the way in which assimilative desires and love of copia coexist in that literature with other, more centripetal impulses, and especially the way in which notions of subjectivity exist on the cusp between them. Or, as the "couplet" of sonnet 126 of *Shake-speares Sonnets* would have it:

"(   )
 (   )"

Architecture

Once there was a future when we were very young.

What remains is tied to us with a barely visible whirring—
      through which birds now slip rapidly
one by one, between the narrow meanings

given in our disarming dream.

      A hole is cut into the wind as the body takes
its leave—witnesses transcribing what they see—
      a fabric of leaves caught up
in a branch.

      Nightly trains drop their cargo in this city
we know, *in which we have never lived*, the river flashing
      and flowing on as our late plural,
below the colonnades, arches, latticework, and windows.

The past goes by loudly on a side street and someone,
      the future insists, is rising, rising—
myth's claim upon us? *Meanwhile*,

she was still looking, looking and longing for her.
      Lost in that upswing of birds,
they'll arrive in separate descriptions as the late afternoon
      rings out its sharp X.
         Once there were the bells.

One of them slowly rows the boat out: bread, salt, wine
      appear in the hull. *What of the sea?*
(As if, in the intervening years, there had been no depletion
      of desire.) The other, meanwhile,
listens for those *wordes* and then (*hear the chant?*)

      for an ancient grammar to arrange
the communal. Meanwhile and *meanwhile*—
      light and its split surface
(columns, domes and canals, the intricate fences).

White Flowers

white lights, white noise and white punctuation marks,
analogies of the clear robe in which I will dress

waiting for an open bridge to take me back to the faceless
world. What I've held in my hands (knives, some nails,

that gift of cool peaches out of season) textures a host
of unformed words in my mouth. Large paper flowers

rustle in a design of coloration which continues
from one life into the next. Enter the nine young

girls who, in those few burning months before
becoming women, hide in a circle of articulation.

(They left Ophelia's wet path from the river
strewn with trillium.) And when my turn comes,

they'll enter my room and casually, knowingly
change certain facts in my past, letting out

their wet hair and laughing aloud into my sleep.

Night Blindness

Beneath any common belief
lies the unspoken, occluded, torn
way we proceed. (On the beach
we were washed clean by transverse
waves). All day long, on these
two lanes, gulls let clams and other
mollusks drop from their beaks—
the animals, raw, inside—
(At first, black sinew held fast
the hinge on each shattered,
calcareous shell). Then we
were driving between dunes
(riding time) on a glacial carved
landscape—out to Race Point—
much as a word travels through
the sensorial inner ear to the cranial
space. Now satellites transmit
the originating explosion, traced
in the fossil radiation, an echo
of singularity carried on rip-tides
of electromagnetic waves—
carrying forth the broken symmetry—
And no rain in weeks.
A chalky road illuminates
a place.

The Lighthouse

i.

Impatient with spring's incendiary budding, we longed for the irreconcilable tossing of summer's phenomenal vowels: brief cawing from gulls on the pilings to divide and overturn May's minor successes (that profusion of greens rubbing against the loosened pane). We watched as an afternoon was laid over the afternoons, like rain on the sea. Renting one of the many clattering skiffs in which to reach the peninsula, we traversed an idea of space and saturation all the way out to where the phosphorous shards of early evening grew hard with a deepening friction. Occasionally the lacunae between stars would glow dimly—stars which became, under different names each night, our ardent relief—a cool and continuous wake left by scores of April violets.

ii.

More than a pyrrhic discovery—clusters of Queen Anne's lace through which the wind inscribes a muted text. Salt air burns the last of winter's damp cordwood to ash. The weathervane spins inside a set of parallel winds. By our road, the heavy monody of goldenrod. The first June lily opened its whitest furl—the field itself in an hour of heliotropic origin. After that, we liked the way the tight equation of waves went on finishing nothing among the many drifts of seaweed swaying all day at the fray.

iii.

Of the types of inflorescence, she liked compound umbel and corymb best—wild carrot and cherry—variation of structuring root, pith and stem. What became of the leaky skiff, its aluminum tuned to thinness by this water's relentless logarithm? The days themselves became fractions of polished metal, tuneless numbers, as the acute and accurate boat was worn away by reference, and by our other forms of luminous inquiry. The bay dispersed the heat of our instincts until the boat became the question of a transparency gained through travel. So long exposed to those elemental particulars, the boat is hard to conceive of—moving as it does between one ideal shore and another—just an inference of relation with seldom a trace to be spoken of. Then, just an open sea to hold the boat's oscillations, the echoes of its cold-burning song.

iv.

It was the effort of sifting through August's scattered abeyance which awakened our love of autumn's delay—that voice of its tonal gesture in a phonemic drift through which vowels were only so many moorings—boats in the harbor. Every so often the gulls' pitch reduced the day's amplitude to fractions of its blue equation, leaving the wooden piles of consonants with which our nights were built. Not the view, but the window glass (long past molten) was our perspective on this sea's refracting tones. Outside, a wind's thin tremolo through dunes would light or delay our sleep. We knew how suddenly the idea of a more distant paradise leaves you.

Architecture (II)

Assurances—the way, in our absence, things repair themselves:
    the old barn leaning, birds nesting, allowing a common good
        to arrive sometime after. All along, a life
            of endless etceteras.

Can music be split open to reveal cosmologies—
    something about generations of families and the end
        of eras? Then one reaches to turn off the tape,
            getting up for a brief walk.

What then is the purpose of measuring this world through reason?
    At the end (smooth finish of the quartet) only
        more particles—still *divisible*—then sadness,
            and no questions anymore.

And the tongue then burneth fiercely, and the parched throat is inflamed:
    the beauty of the eyes . . .When is one no longer listening
        to a fleeting sound (to intervals of distance)
            or those distances between?

In longitudinal waves I've learned to hear a displacement
    increasing between the compression and the rarefaction:
        all through this darkness structured more fully than light,
            space and time beating level,

and corresponding only to the diamond in the eye.

Apophatic

Low-tide shoals flat-lit
and contused.

The night's bittersweet and phosphorous
like a gravitational imprint

(force and matter no different in the end . . .)

Traffic's quarrying its margin—
all arrival and Lethean assemblage—

antiparticles ribbing the ink-wet shallows
(earlier, in daylight, a squall of gulls)

Blacker now, until the mild stars begin
to turn inside the nonluminous matter—

in the governing sea of neutrinos—

     *

(Stay awhile in me)
(*All that I ask is that my error last* . . .)

     *

In the void
some sacrifice—

some wildness beginning
to thrive—

     *

I watch the tide drift into partitions,
mutely in the marshes—

its absorption and dispossession
of the inlet, the stars, the palisade

of cars starting up around me—

     *

Then a gale, all edge and factual
aftermath,

begins over the buoys and wild
hibiscus

(replicas in an ocean's slur and graphitic
wreckage—

*that immersion in which you were always
lost to me—)*

and then over the waters of the earth which will not
remember us.

Vigil

midnight never falls at midnight
—Blanchot

I.

Dissimulation's inside
the song too.

A letter darkness
in spring's

cold reparations.
A troubled hindrance.

Wind pours its verdigris
favor.

I choose its parceled
intercession,

its tattered, insistent
configuration with all

its devotions gone—

all the dialectics and names—
in shallow evaporation.

II.

Intractable, gleaming
subjugation of day

and night, caught
in the rock and pitch

past grief and its lack:
an entwined wheel

railing through absolute
and unturned waves.

No minor wind.
No interval

in the graven sleep
to burnish

or resemble
this famished

mourning
for disavowal—

adamantine
decorum—

oblivion's hive.

III.

Then an inscription on the catastrophe.
Late shade and ash in the day telling
of an obverse name spelled out in air.
(We're there, in its scarce elaboration,
one vowel darker than another.)
On the beach, I hear a blunt edge
of wind and waves in brief convolution,
their axial dominions of symmetry
and brittle shell mouthing the closed
syllables of earth's continents—
a volcano's deep echo from the boat's keel—

MICHELE GLAZER

ARTIST'S STATEMENT

I write what bothers me. A phrase drifts in, maybe a rhythm, a feeling or an image carries sufficient ballast and dangles a loose end. I suppose my poems come out of a desire for something hard and irrefutable coupled with a distrust of absolutes in just about every realm.

That there is for me no inherent purpose in life is not necessarily a frightening proposition. But it puts the burden on language—syntax, rhythm, images, architectures—

I love the feeling of being lost in something, of making an object, usually by slow accretion, from material I had not known would combine, of following language to something that has a shape—which is a kind of meaning. I would admit too that silence has always been for me a little too easy to keep, and too difficult to live in.

Charles Simic said, in describing a prose poem, "[it's] a bit like trying to catch a fly in a dark room. The fly probably isn't even there, the fly is inside your head, still, you keep tripping over and bumping into things in hot pursuit. The prose poem is a burst of language following a collision with a large piece of furniture." I like this awkward bumping into things and the exhilarating rush of language; at the same time I am drawn to silence, the silence after exhaustion or before utterance. It is lyrical, with a knife. In my work I want the sense of mass and energy suggested by Simic's description to meet the stark lyricism of a kind of silence. What planet would that be?

What I do: A significant percentage of beetles that feed at flowers eat pollen and some even chew on the flower itself. Despite the damage they can cause with their rummaging, some pollen sticks to their bodies. This is called *mess and soil pollination*.

What I don't try to do is write to demystify or even, exactly, to understand. Nor do I write to make things strange, but my experience is that the longer I look at something, the stranger it turns out to be. I'm thinking not only of the

47

profound disjunction between language and the material world, but also of the real strangeness of the material world. What I want to do, and syntax may be where I lean the hardest, is to try to make of language an object so lyrical in its discordances that it cracks open.

Influences:

"*So*" was a word I heard often growing up. Not in conjunction with two ideas in a yoke of logic, but as a "turn-out," sending the dangerous train in the direction of safety or to silence. But.

Nature as utterly other. As other people are too sometimes.

The mountains and dark forests of the Northwest.

Not to put too fine a point on imagery.

All That in the Voice I Have Adopted for This Lie

(for J. K.)

Fresh figs blacken and sweeten.
The Mediterranean sun lengthens and roots,
tipped by a nimble surer than a dowser's wand, sink
like the dream into the dreamer.
On top a woman walks about.
To wend the invisible is to know
the obstacle before they meet.
She knows these leaves
are fleshy with an inference
she restrains herself from touching and feels lush
in her restraint.
Too-sweet, the figs
rot.

      She's had enough, she knows what they are doing,
roots waking to receding water.
Naked, in the shower, and her feet, naked too, of course, she stands
inches deep in the brackish back-up, the color swirling —no
no-color— it's the shadow
cast by water,
an appalling and miraculous
root-soup.

      They are waking and she knows it.
There is no wobble down there.
All direction is toward desire
if desire's felt. How often she is
two ways at once.
She is old and bends
easily. She is thin.
She is on her knees, with both hands
she wends the snake down in.

"The Purpose of Design Is to Make the Whole Greater Than the Sum of Its Parts"

1)
That red-shafted flicker in the woods.
    Is it the one you claimed
Probed the one oak? Can you hear it?

    Decay has its own
Small life; the bird heard
    It and, entering, turned it

From abstraction into flesh.

1)
If long ago we made things longer
    By piecing the parts together, then
Whole years passed this way
    And that.

1)
What is *in*
    To a hole any flicker might
Slip through?

1)
The oak died and the bird didn't kill it.

1)
One hole nearly fills this scab
    Of bark. And the hole
Insists, doesn't it,
    On a *here* and a *there*
Out of the air. But your mouth

Wraps around a sound
    That will not let you out.

    If I could piece the parts . . . , part

With the pieces . . .

1)

> *Lay down your head now don't you*
> *Feel almost at home?*

1)

One gnat to
Whom fine mesh may be
Invisible will fill an eye.
What blunders—
Your good blue eye it drowns
In, too large
To see.

1)
And this isn't about
You, really, what
Is?

Science

Larkspur—bluemoss—his deciduous hands—
oh, but why would you want to?
He is somber honey.
He is a mouthful of bees.

2 Blinds & a Bittern

Among bitterns one is blind.

Among reeds, bittern is the middle swayer.

In the blind I am all eyes.

To the eye on the other side I am

abstract, an eye, too, and green

but nothing

to beat your wings about.

The blind offered itself as a way to see

deeper into what out there

kept at abeyance, us.

Still, when we were happy we forgot ourselves . . . . . . something like that.

Who watches for what moves

and what sits

still among the rushes?

And where the branch

meets the bird.

I didn't say I was interested in the birds, particularly,

I just said I couldn't find them.

In the blind we are all eyes and I

am the middle swayer.

In the blind we pull birds out of the sky with other birds

we work *like puppets*

into the net between the firs.

This blind runs Cooper's hawks—

the blind with the rain gutter and the burlap-covered boards.

There is concern about the bird whose tail lacks rigidity.

The lure-birds ride pulleys—pigeon, dove, English sparrow.

They wear leather vests and precious little else.

Someone bolts for the caught hawk, checks it for crop, for molt, for parasites, the wing pit for fat. Opens the hatch.

It's easy to love a thing against the sky but you can't just look at one thing and say, "oh, it's a redtail."   It has to all add up.

Wherein space is constructed
that matter may reside in . . .

The weather forecast that snow would fall from the sky.

(The architecture of snow was like the architecture

of the storm itself, and of the landscape.)

The weather forecast *was* that snow would fall.

We are like snow he said.

She understood her heart was cold.

And that if the walls could not be breached by rhetoric

or conjecture, still they leaned, comfortably

perhaps, one against the other,

an aggregate of disturbances, as rust

that in the meantime corrodes, makes beautiful.

You are like snow. She thought,

but I told you that before.

The architecture of loss, the hand of a loved one.

You are not like other weather he said.

Matter

i.

The pronghorn's all four legs had caught in the fence & it had worn one
    side of its face
smooth in the dirt trying to separate its flesh from the barbed wire. It was
    moving
& if the struggle was for the mother whose footprint we had seen earlier or
    for the juniper
here & there or the vastness of sagebrush it was also about pain & the
    certainty
of metal that seized as the animal shrank against large birds circling in the
    sky & coyotes
& from the sun. Anyone looking down would have wondered
that the animal should fear things circling & round. By *worn its face smooth*
I mean rubbed the hair off.

It had been all day without water & the dirt, too, is worn smooth here
    where the head rubbed over it.

It wasn't a pronghorn but an elk & the eye was clear water silted over & the
    shape of itself.
It was the content of another.

But then it is back to the garden, you see, where everything grows
with such fecundity (witness the rampant mint) that she must be
constantly pulling up & putting everything into it & everything
has begun to feel like

more, she puts herself into it.

ii.

The comeupon head of the baby goat was glossy white, a kind of third-
world neon because this was Kathmandu & walking by looking back
didn't clarify whether it was the real head or why its eyes looked
moist but I got it

the head that had been part of the animal—now a window
advertisement for its own dismembered parts.

box

rather a box of winds
than a sack, then

my heart's carapace.
am rust. anointed

danger, nature, lust.
rather for what?

am stall, then.
rather, a sack of winds.

who trusts in god knows
dumb luck's

other half
that startles, starts.

inside the box the god in truss.
rather the river than the rock

the river breaks on
that sack of winds, like something

I whispered into
your ear nothing

was said.

Echo to Narcissus

Nature drives me crazy, how it repeats.
Yet I love pattern as I love a promise,
to think that what will follow is something
I can know. How ring for ring the oak grows.
And I in felling it repeat the blows. Narcissus,
pattern weds us. And he says "no."

She answers *no.*

Sonnet

*The threatened vernal pool fairy shrimp is a 3/4-inch translucent crustacean
with a one-year life cycle and a unique survival strategy.*

Invisible in vernal pools—
the fairy shrimp have no secrets.
But if their bodies are—in water—
as transparent as desire what
can desire hold?
This close to bodiless—what they possess
they will not have and what's seen-
through seems only there by her
imagining them. So that later
when his fingers touched her navel—*I'll kiss you
there, only*—is what he said and let his mouth roam
up to where the quartermoon of one breast
quieted him, she could feel how he had practiced
this before with his eyes closed   and alone.

Early Romance, Japanese Garden
(*in the heart of the city*)

We sit on a bench & look at the raked rocks:
The islands of Japan. The improbable waves.

Map

Everywhere there was a bush and a bird in it.

Things popped out of the grasses

clicking and you knew

you were walking in nature, entering Brush Canyon

exiting Bird so I kept thinking why

should I be the one always asking where it hurts?

Somewhere we paused where

a plank got wedged between trees,

tight so we could sit on it. I touched the wound

—that something viscous

could be pitch at an attitude that hard.

Where Bird Canyon was subsumed by Bear Gulch

the one I was with peeled off to shortcut up some shortcut

so I walked up Downey Gulch through a saw of indolent cows.

I knew them for what they were—red eyes, bulk

and jitteriness—

the way it's always something.

For the first time it was clear to me

that the lines on my map were the draws

and gullies I was lost in

so I couldn't stay lost. That night the sky was nothing

but stars and the crickets made a curtain of sound.

Why can't I remember that? He washed my hair.

I lay on the porch with my neck extended; he rested

my head in his open hand. The sky had rounded

up all its citizens and pressed down.

MaTTHea Harvey

arTIST's statemenT

Wouldn't it be wonderful if we could put on Cézanne spectacles and see exactly what he saw? Representation (be it poetry or the visual arts) is always, to some extent, a distortion. You see a red shirt. I see a bird. A number of the poems in my first book, *Pity the Bathtub Its Forced Embrace of the Human Form,* explore the process of painting, which is itself another few steps up the kitchen path away from the washing line where there's either a shirt hanging or a cardinal perched. Add to that the fact that many of the artworks discussed in the poems are imaginary, and you get the picture. The distance becomes the subject of the poem.

Though I would claim Emily Dickinson (interior decorator of the mind) and Wallace Stevens (titler extraordinaire—how I envy "Le Monocle de Mon Oncle") as my primary parents in the poetic pantheon, I go to the work of artists like Agnes Martin and Rebecca Horn and (graphic) artists Chris Ware and Peter Blegvad to open up my eyes. My aim is to be un-innocently wide-eyed, a receptive detective, a Matthea with antennae.

A number of the poems in *Pity the Bathtub Its Forced Embrace of the Human Form* use what I call "swivel lines" or "hinges." In these poems, the last word of a sentence is also the first word of the next phrase, creating a magnetic enjambment which holds the poems together, keeps them from flying apart. These poems are manic mouthfuls, afraid of silence. The "forced embrace" of this form is meant to mimic the uneasy fit of the body within the bathtub, the "self" within the body.

I take the simple machine aspect of the hinge lines a step further in my second book, *Sad Little Breathing Machine,* which explores the various systems we live amongst, under and in between. I examine these systems from three vantage points: through introduction poems, engine poems (some of which have explicit engines and others that take their titles for their engines), and prose poems.

In "Introduction to Eden" (one of nine introduction poems that divide the book), the garden of Eden is imagined as a system *literally* in dialogue with humans. The system begins speaking and the human voice (a collective "we") tries to engage with and understand the terms of the conversation. The language of the "we" alters as it learns these terms, and can express (in a way the system understands) rebellion, play, or pleas. The engine poems are systems themselves. These poems often have what I call an "engine" in the epigraph position beneath the title. The engines are sometimes visual diagrams (as in "Engine: @" or "Engine: → ←!"), sometimes phrases, and sometimes both. The engine serves as the guiding force behind each poem's movement—in effect it "runs" the poem. The engines' workings are not explicit, instead they provide a ghost of order in the same way that we see a car move and do not always know exactly what is going on under the hood. Meanwhile, the prose poems are explicit in precisely the way the engine poems are not. They wear theories and thinking on the outside as opposed to the inside, like a see-through watch. Each poem is based on one simple idea out of which a narrative and miniature world is spun.

I'm always looking to invent or discover new structures in language to get my poems closer to wonder. As Dada poet Hugo Ball said, "Why can't a tree be called Pluplusch, and Pluplubasch when it has been raining?"

Translation

They see a bird that is bright in both beak and feather
And call it cardinal not thinking to import the human
Kind words welcome those who stumble to shore
With the tilt of the sea still in their step salt stains
At their hems that seem to map out coastlines left far
Behind the new songs are the old absurd hopes
A woman wiping the table sings *bring me plans*
And money or fans and honey each word more
Strange yellow flowers spring up in the first lawns
Instead of white dots of daisies how to tell what is
A weed is persistent and is to be emulated says a man
In a tavern in church the preacher lectures on Lazarus
Gesturing wildly as another boatload lurches along
A latitude is a guiding line a platitude a boring line
Chorus the children in school their slates scrawled
And smudged with sums that always seem to come to
Nothing is quite the same here a woman writes a letter
Near the lighthouse but the fog is so thick the words
Run as she writes them for a moment she can't tell
The sea spray from the fog one falls back the other stays
Suspended between two houses in the distance is a
Clothesline with a red shirt on it but she sees a bird

Nude on a Horsehair Sofa by the Sea

I don't know what to do with his body.
It looks smooth—& heavy too—
from the way the sofa's mahogany claws
sink into the sand. Every other wave
is brown, the ones in between a light liquor
bottle green, & the strip of wet sand
the froth laps, then leaves, is glass-
brown & shouldn't act like mud
but does. When a seagull struts by
I see the others flick their brushes
in irritation over that spot as if to
drive it away—& me, I'm avoiding
the subject, still fretting over how to paint
the word *sometimes* because the pebbles
only show when the water's had a chance
to settle. I can tell he's secretly moving
his toes along the grain of the sofa
& back, so the hairs lie smooth, then
bristle as one wave crests & another
crashes. The woman next to me sighs.
Her clouds look like dark whales floating
in the sky, her brush hovers over
them then dips down to make
an awkward dab at the spot between
the model's thighs. It is starting
to drizzle now & each wave has a pocked
& peaked landscape of its own & people
are folding their easels & shielding
their paintings with their bodies as they run
to the striped cabanas. Perhaps he will whisk
out a cloak & wade slowly into the water,
silk billowing about his fine white ankles.
Perhaps he has to help carry the sofa. I turn
and trudge after the others, picking a path
through the driftwood littered like collarbones
on the beach. I want a way to take it all
with me—the sag of the sofa beneath him &
the curve of the ocean which is what I think
the iris must look like from inside the eye.

The Festival of Giovedo Grasso

Because it means looking into the sun, people can barely see
    the two boys in the belltower or the two cables running
from it to the ground. One boy crouches in a boat without oars,
    the other hangs from a harness in the next archway over,
ready to jump. He doesn't have wings, but he is cherubic, picked
    for his wide eyes and smooth cheeks. As he falls he holds
the bouquet the way he's been told to—far out in front of him
    so it looks like a message from God. And in case
the image isn't enough, there's the boy in the boat, tossing
    interpretation into the crowds. If the boat wobbles instead
of gliding, it's because he has to get the last few pamphlets
    and poems out from under his feet. No gold unless
the gondola is empty when he lands. He is lucky. It is windy
    and the words go far. Together their descents form
two arms of a compass. Between them, as if they had drawn it,
    the piazza. Must it mean something if two boys who fall
from the same spot land in opposite corners? Must there always
    be a lesson? To me it looks like a diagram of the distance
between what we believe and what we do, but it doesn't hold
    my attention. The crowd is cheering as the boat's bottom
scrapes along the stones; the other boy is handing over his
    flowers even before his heels hit the ground.
Dogs are leaping around the fountain with poems in their mouths
    and the sun slips down the churchsteps one by one.

Thermae

I don't have a bath every day. The water bites into you, and as the days go by, your heart turns to water.—Petronius

I. Vestibulum (entrance hall)

Because he is thinking so hard about his ode, because his mind is full of *what if I fail, what if I can't imagine it* he doesn't notice the man with the ill-fitting toga in front of him whom he would have mocked at dinner— twisting his napkin around his fingers to demonstrate—or the man lurking in a portico, clearly a thief, watching the lines of people fingering their fee. The wait does not seem long to him. Usually he would be peering up at the frescos, trying to let their brightness into him—he'd be dizzy by the time it came to pay—but because now he is trying to reconcile *naval battle* and *just for show*, he barely notices when it's his turn and the attendant has to take the gold coin from him.

II. Apodyterium (dressing room)

Constellations in the corners. Having unwound their masters' togas the servants hold the wide white circles out in front of their bodies—their dark heads like planets revolving around a moon. Then they fold the moon. Someone here must have seen one of the Naumachiae he thinks as he slips off his tunic, winds his belt around it, and stows the unwieldy scroll. Since he has to worry about it being stolen, he's wearing the wine-stained one, frayed at the hem with an occasional hole. This is not how he dresses for Fortunata who spends two hours each morning fussing with her hair. It was her idea that he come here today, but so far inspiration has not struck. He studies the men's foreheads trying to see waves in the wrinkles, sun-glints and boats in the flecks of their eyes.

III. Palaestra (athletics room)

O fickle muse, feather ball tossed between men, you come when you want to and never for long. Three men are playing at it, hitting the ball with their palms, softly, as if they don't really want to push it away. Its slow floating is a form of gloating. The arcs their arms make in the air look like entranceways, but their tunics stick to their chests. The ball falls to the floor, a servant picks it up, they begin again. Others roll silver hoops and run after them. The wrestlers require no intermediaries. Naked but for a film of wax and dust, they flex their muscles and slip around like fish, grinding dirt into the bright mosaic floor. If it were that easy. If you could wrestle it down.

IV. Laconicum (sweating room)

Steam makes a dream-scene out of the sweating men. He doesn't know if what beads on his skin comes from in him or from the air. What he does know: sometimes they would flood an existing arena, sometimes they built a lake especially for the battle. Sea animals were put in the water to make it more real. Eels definitely. Surely no sharks. He'd like to include a narwhal, its spiral tusk an element of chance in the planned choreography, but he's not sure his patron will agree. Should he stick to facts when he has so few? Scent of olive oil and musk in the air, servants scraping their masters' skin with strigils until told to stop. He rubs his back against a marble wall.

V. Calidarium (hot room)

He will focus on a woman. Always a good idea. Where shall she sit? In the first row of seats, water lapping below her feet. Maybe she sips from a green goblet, makes the scene even stranger by looking through it and cheering for the most wildly tinted men. Predictably her lover favors the Athenians. She doesn't mind the blood, has seen it all before, but she enjoyed the lion eating the ostrich more. No. Odes should exalt. Begin again. Perhaps she is Fortunata minus the moles, less likely to lecture. Mentally, he gives her the same pretty nose, a few extra charms, then goes to the bronze basin in the middle of the room, splashes scalding water onto his face and arms. For the more modest there are separate baths along the walls. Studying them he decides to use stanzas.

VI. Tepidarium (warm room)

With his toe he traces the arabesques from the walls onto the bottom of the bath. Here, everyone is the same height, a head above water, their bodies gangly shadows below. This would be the time to ask someone: A man falls from his replica-ship and drowns. Is he dead then or only when the drama is over—the arena drained and he's found pale and bloated on the floor? It is hard enough to imagine the furnaces beneath the bath— people fanning them, feeding them—or the network of aqueducts criss- crossing the countryside to bring water to this particular silver spout, let alone trying to puzzle out what the eye sees when told *this is the battle* but knows it's not. To him similes seem more scrupulous. Aqueducts act like ideas, but not exactly.

VII. Frigidarium (cold room)

Rain comes in through the oculus making a splashing circle the swimmers avoid. Without the sun the hall is very dark, very cold. He considers not getting in, but his only alternative is to walk home in the wet. From here he can see part-way into the unctuarium—an oiled body shakes under a masseuse's pummeling. Another is picking a perfume. These are the men who will be wrapped in silk, escorted to their litters, carried away without their feet ever touching the streets. He shivers, jumps in, starts swimming. When his fingers hit the pool-end he surfaces. His hair, brown and curly before, is sleek. Squint and he might be the figure he will describe at the start of his poem—Triton, man from the waist up, fish from the waist down, a heart that can't tell the difference.

Image Cast by a Body Intercepting Light

Shadows simplify—the beak combing the back is lost
    in the outlines of the body, the outstretched wing
a sharp shape, featherless, against next-door's brick.
    The light hits so that the shadow birds on shadow wire
slant diagonally while their more creaturely counterparts perch
    on a prim perpendicular. Dreams refract and flatten
this way, changing the postman into "the one who will deliver,"
    letting a lover repent, but in a silly suit in the supermarket.
Ambition also—a man plans his fruit orchards, discovers too late
    he owns acres of rock. It isn't the light that sets him to
tunneling, it's revision of sorts. Now he imagines his groves in
    caves where he can control the sunlight through skylights,
direct one ray at each ripening fruit. Lemons, oranges, limes,
    they flourish down there, nourished below by what would
have gnarled them above. Picture him strolling proudly overhead,
    watching his shadow slipping in between the trees. How could
it not please him to see another figure there, following his footsteps
    inexactly? He begins to think of marriage, of children filling
the caverns with laughter and perhaps for one moment he considers
    the order of creation—that God made the sun and made us after.

One Filament against the Firmament

Most days Group V. practiced on seeing through
Prisms because of the way they bend the light
They are considered the first marker of advanced
Sight tests had been conducted on them all as
Children these ones could examine a dewdrop
Perched on a furred leaf and not cry when it fell to
The ground had no more data to give though later
The books would be buried to give us something new
To discover God could not be a matter of spaceships
The way must be found through the mind and the
Eyes are distractible as the Leader discovered one night
In a stairwell when one lightbulb overhead managed
To distract him from the sky outside he decided
That finding beauty pointless might actually be the
Point at something and then see past it became
The first lesson to lessen attachment to things put
Here to distract us of course there were detractors
Who thought the fingers or tongue would work just
Fine lines of personality scar the fingertips though
And tastebuds cannot belie their bias only the mind
And the eyes could absorb indefinitely pupils practiced
Not shrinking at the sun it was an honor to go blind
Trying to ignore the tiny creatures that float across
Our eyes was a task that drove hundreds crazy because
It didn't make sense that something tiny and see-through
Could lure the gaze away from the Taj Mahal or a Monet
Which they practiced in front of because of the lovely
Colors and affection for them were eliminated later as were
All forms of luxury like being able to see your family
Across the breakfast table they all disappeared one by
One day everybody woke up alone and couldn't find
Each other and they all would have died from standing
Still there was one girl who hadn't been able to stop loving
The word marshmallow and one boy who still had a favorite
Color slowly seeped back into the world and a new group
Formed to research why it had left but it never became clear

The Crowds Cheered as Gloom Galloped Away

Everyone was happier. But where did the sadness go? People wanted to know. They didn't want it collecting in their elbows or knees then popping up later. The girl who thought of the ponies made a lot of money. Now a month's supply of pills came in a hard blue case with a handle. You opened it & found the usual vial plus six tiny ponies of assorted shapes & sizes, softly breathing in the styrofoam. Often they had to be pried out & would wobble a little when first put on the ground. In the beginning the children tried to play with them, but the sharp hooves nicked their fingers & the ponies refused to jump over pencil hurdles. The children stopped feeding them sugarwater & the ponies were left to break their legs on the gardens' gravel paths or drown in the gutters. On the first day of the month, rats gathered on doorsteps & spat out only the bitter manes. Many a pony's last sight was a bounding squirrel with its tail hovering over its head like a halo. Behind the movie theatre the hardier ponies gathered in packs amongst the cigarette butts, getting their hooves stuck in wads of gum. They lined the hills at funerals, huddled under folding chairs at weddings. It became a matter of pride if one of your ponies proved unusually sturdy. People would smile & say, "this would have been an awful month for me," pointing to the glossy palomino trotting energetically around their ankles. Eventually, the ponies were no longer needed. People had learned to imagine their sadness trotting away. & when they wanted something more tangible, they could always go to the racetrack & study the larger horses' faces. Gloom, #341, with those big black eyes, was almost sure to win.

Introduction to Eden

Call me What You Will.

This for your complicated hands—
my best mechanical tree.

Test?   No thank you.
Question?   The rivers run in circles.
You noticed.   We noticed.

(thinking)

Duet!   & the pin factory . . .

Sweet extrovert, it is making pins

You will, you know,
but I shouldn't sing   Introvert! Introvert!
if I were you

in case the gate sings back.

JOAN HOULIHAN

ARTIST'S STATEMENT

The Pleasure Principle

A poem is not a polemic, it is a pleasure—or it should be. The ways in which a poem imparts pleasure include originality (and accuracy) of image and metaphor, fresh use of language, and, especially, music—the sound and rhythm in its lines. Deeper pleasures accrue when the poem also has surprise and subtlety of meaning, deeper still when it has coherence, when the marks of an organizing intelligence are all over it like fingerprints.

Writing a poem is a deliberate and daring act, where the multiplicity of the self seizes for once its own best order and speaks from it fearlessly, inscribing its moment in the sun in the reader's mind. It is deliberate and it is personal—it is, in fact, an act of love.

For such an act to succeed, for it to impress, affect, and genuinely move another person, there must be a face to meet another face, an "I" to meet another "I"; in short, a self, consistent and coherent, standing like the Wizard of Oz behind the curtain of the poem. Fragmentation thrills, but only against the knowledge of something whole. Mystery delights, but only against the certainty of eventual resolution. And, while the detachment of meaning from language proves the arbitrariness of both, it is merely a proof—and a proof that only needs to be demonstrated once.

I think also a poem must honor its maker, be the maker's emissary to the reader, announcing without apology and with passion what is individual, unique, and alive. Certainly, there are poets who have sent such emissaries to me. For her mastery of craft, I would cite Plath as an influence; for his ecstasy of music, Hopkins; for her introspective fire and honesty, Dickinson; and for his unfettered indulgence in language, imagination, and humor, Ashbery.

Therefore, my aim as a poet is simple—to write a poem that seizes the best self in its moment and that answers the question *who cares?* while also giving the reader the pleasure of its company. Then to write another.

Biological Imperative

The wings suffer most. They stop shining.
A tilt of a nest, a backyard birch
black-sutured, half-dying—for this

we are bound to prepare. I am arrowed to you,
as if born of you, infrared in my bed of slosh
and song. The trajectory of us

can't be stopped. All the dead hum backwards
in the pretty spiral arm of their home.
Degradation: the white of their passing on.

H. Antecessor

All halted elegance, you make a paper wolf for me
then blow into a bottle for the howl. We are so merry
in the belly of July, knees pressed together, kissing

as we eat, while west, in Gran Dolina, the intact
skeletons are spread with tools around a cold hearth.
Trouble yourself: they are deformed

by a hammering for marrow along the longer
bones, and on the templar, blackened for the pot.
When man is a study of tooth mark and fracture,

woman should be wary. I am not. Cloud-tails float
high, uncombed, as I, with found weed braided
simply in my hair, lean to your mouth.

Ardor

I arrive to you as rain does:
sudden as a flung robe
and urgent.

Let down the scarf
along your hair.

At the window, horses stand in a circle
calmed by hay, their rainy hides
releasing a snuffed ancestry.

Turned out and without
such fortitude we will diminish—
unfairness of limbs, shrunken

valves unable to pump,
wind-crossed and in postures
modest and stooped.

There is only one way to speak of this:
as of a joy no longer curable.

And Everywhere Offering Human Sound

Come here. Let me finger your hair.
I like the way you imitate weather:
a white breath, here and there,
the rush and sting of pinkened air,
a coven of crows talking briefly of home
and then the pelted tree.
By these shall I know ye,
bless yer little round mug.

Oh, my semi-precious, so much slow time
so much crawling and browsing
so much fascination with harmful insects
and corrosive sublimate.
As if you have as many eyes
as many eyes as the common fly,
and every one stuck open wide
to the wonderful, wonderful world.

So, I get up at 4 AM, finally, to put on some tea—
a soothing explanation for steam.
Children grow into themselves, then away.
We mustn't worry when they're gone—
or worse, not-quite-gone-yet.
The roots of things connect
where we can't see.

When I was born, *my* mother began counting
to herself. Something in the middle
must have gone missing.
Fortunately, I have all my faculties.
In fact, I still remember to turn
every small thing until it gleams:
like your favorite airplane pin

there, riding on its own cotton wad.
Now come here so I can see
through your eyes to the sky within.

You are my only animal—
my animal of air.

Matter

I make a little mother out of mud, sticks
and a bit of gauze. Once formed and dried,
she's bound to disappear: powder to my fingers.
All my plaster saints go down that way.
Wormwood. Gall. Sheer age.

Not that it matters, but
I once saw Mars through a telescope:
pockmarked, awash in gas, but distant enough
to have dignity. All this farawayness has to stop.
So much homesickness, but so little home

and so many notions they call tradition.
Knife, fork, whip of potatoes—all the womanly arts
are not so much lost, as far, as spilled
as if moved from the table too fast—
salt from a lidless box. And the one candle

I molded and set on the mantle had to be lit.
To enjoy the burning, Mother said.
Because something holy was happening then,
and all was made to be blown away—burn of cry,
steam of want—expelled like a mouthful of air.

The Infant Spouse

Built and placed it in my body.
Mole-sized, with a lung. Put ear to it
and listened long. Made mouth on it
for suckling. Made fists of cloth
and lickings for it, wax
for where the milktooth bites.
Scoured the wood around the crib,
sacred for the kneeling.

When the surge and bulge began,
I rose it up and circled it
with ropy cord, to isolate. Came with bowls
of flaring oils—first to light, then feed it.
Always starving for me, staring,
numinous, attaching.

Never without tremble
or wet breath, following half-visibly,
a crippled luminosity. On Memorial Drive
I see it—steady as an alcoholic.
I call to it, take it home
and tend its cratered heat.
What will I do without it, when alone.

Squall Line

In the farther sky rain gathers.
The smell is nickel. I long to replenish,

lean out like a dog, mouth sprung, tongue
loose, lapping the mineral air

because I must. In the quick theater
of highway, a low bird

sidles to his bleed of meat.
Too bad. I've never been bitten—

only struck solemn, as in a funeral parlor
where the body is lit from above. Clouds bloat

the horizon. *Let's go back*, I say,
to the other version of us. But we are taken

with the scramble of rain over weed, over
bed-rolled hay—the decant of all missed things.

Incarnation

Brought in by pulling you under the arms
as one would a carnal bulk or bagged weight.

Brought in from an unsheltered water.
Brought in from a lanterned shore, and left

the way a tide is, continuous and without intent.
A downing of air then finger to lip pronounced you

gone. What's best kept close is this you, tiny—
your bed a fold, a night shell. Your modest need

for rest and food. Your school of injury and singing.
Now we can talk anywhere.

Hydrangeas

Salt air flutters them, cradles
their heads, lolling and solemn

as babies born slow. The heft
and bend is determined by stem;

by water, genetics and sleight of wind.
We left what unsettles us to come here

where the lengthy water unstops and spills,
mottled by sunset, crossed by gull,

immortality's waves in a chamber of skull.
The children grow hairy and tall as they sleep.

Loose boats are bruising the dock.
What the sea dredges up in the dark

this time, is sand tooth, spine, effacement of rock—
hard fruit of the tide, left where it's dropped.

Unnestled, we listen to salt air drift
across the hydrangeas; its shift.

All the Cold Mechanicals

As the hill assumed its dome of snow
and the least frozen thing its life,
I assumed us. Winter singed over
with cryable light as we sped downhill,
stung fresh, tucked in. I granted sky
its steeling cloud, its lance of branches,
darker where we landed, snow most chaste
where legs and arms imprinted shapes,
left them diminishing continuously.
Our lightened sleds responded to our tugs
as night delayed by whitened hills—
all the cold mechanicals in place.
How much smaller we've grown, each winter
rising unrefreshed, more empty of us.
Come to the window my childhood friend.
See how the branches are cast in snow again
and freckled over with melting.

CHRISTINE HUME

ARTIST'S STATEMENT

Hume's Theory of the External World, Part I

Houseflies have not been domesticated by humans; rather, they have domesticated themselves in order to live with us. Their devotion is evolutionary—flies are hard-wired to sound like company. And anyone who's ever been trapped in a room with a fly knows: it both always and never seems to be flying toward you; that simultaneous direction and indirection is a poetic triumph. A fly knows how to throw sounds around the room. Montaigne complains that the fly's hissing is enough to murder his mind. If so, then it puts on the dead mind's dress, it addresses us. Its mental flights go off restlessly, intrepidly; it keeps swerving and transforming its flight-line. The fly catches in our bonnets, ruffling the surface of meaning. It whispers harebrained *ahas!*, naked non sequiturs, paralogical postula—assumes a screwy and fantastically sensible distraction from our utilitarian ways with language. Luring us away from the mundane and the hermetic, the fly collects for us an echo chamber of a world outside. It becomes the ghost of language's agitations, an audible ghost clanking about in the attic. A certain insistent rhythm and buzz often kick the poem into being, but they also help it build its own order, its "meter-making argument" (Emerson). My preference for speeding among phonetic associations often shows me an unexpected pattern and logic that shifts the poem's ultimate course. I try to keep the sound going, to see how many sounds can open up possibilities beyond my first impulses. The accrual of design (sonic, imagistic, rhetorical) also allows for electrified mistakes, resonant slippages, kinetic cryptographies, and alchemical transumptions. The poem's sensual speculations excite new knowledges, multiple landings. "And hit a world, at every plunge / And finish knowing—then—" (Dickinson). A fly may cast its gigantic shadow anywhere; its shade may become a place of pleasurable capacity and perversity. Language creates place as much as it does movement—moving forms matter, moving matters form. The places where my work tends to invent substrata ambivalence, and contradiction, where times (tenses) and cultures (mythologies) have been corralled into one untidy spot, collapsed within "the immediate realm of the teletopological present. Here you will experience cartographic failure" (DJ Spooky). Twice winged, compound eyed, the fly crosses through the no-fly zone knowing and not knowing full well.

True and Obscure Definitions
of *Fly*, Domestic and Otherwise

Do what we can, summer will have its flies:
a paper fly cage dangles from the ceiling
a fly on the coach wheel
sent her away with a fly in her ear
That fly setteth her upon corrupt things
—in the ointment, —in the soup, —on the wall, —off the handle
He grasps the wand that causes sleep to fly
an egg deposited in her flesh
hence to taint secretly
the flye-slow houres
In a pianoforte; In a screw-log
Then flyes in his face all his whoring, swearing, and lying
as if such colors could not fly; a fire—
a bar— and a butter—
something used to cover or connect
with fingers: nimble as knapping a fogle with fingers fly
under that name we comprehend all
muscarius or fly-killers
appeared in the fly-state in —time
and the infinite swarms do shine
a —taker, a —maker as in Every man his own fly-maker
a familiar demon; a flatterer
with wings to be twisted by hand
of a limb: there you see this vain and senseless Flyer
a —breeder; a —duster; a —fancier
of money: to be rapidly spent
as in herds of fly-bitten meat
the steamship flying signals of distress
the pains wander, shoot, and fly about
as Friday flies over my outer wall
the high arc of a ball that has been struck
and suspends a belief in speed
in the time when flies are to be met with
in the time when flies trouble the long tails of giraffes
on the fly; of birds: to issue forth in a body
at the entrance of a tent

Immediately when I hear I will fly you a line

Lies Concerning Speed

say a lake decayed: say wind makes a lake of eyes: an eyed lake sees her here: at bottom a lair of cars: broken windshields rise in lambent announcement: lashed and crack attract each other: greenish bubbles microphone her voice: lake of lapped and insides: say it's ventriloquism: against a lake's static: a lotic laziness to list after: look how the stars open frogs: catch a sound to give back in her own voice: say lost red rings, foreign coins, and hair bands: the day face down on a sleeve of swallows: the lake looks hard: shrinking the sky like a muscle: lake of remembering net bones: all the mossy boats marooned: say the way the wind wants it: a shallow mouth trying to dig itself out: but she is built into: is become as sounding glass: lake of stealing and hulls: guess how leaves leave the shapes of wings: a stick bends sound in water: shadows skim the skin debris: mumbling her into shape: say her brain needles when she looks into the edge: lake of dumb and numberless sight: the lucid parts only reflect: still saying how to keep herself overheard: *I could show you myself were I near you*

A Million Futures of Late

There'll be no town-going today;
I'll be wind-rattled and listen
to the window's answering racket.
I'll watch flies manifest from glass
then rub the rust and sadness off.
I'll have my lapses into slapsticks
of accent and stutter, girl and mother.
Flies will spin a crown of woozy cartoon stars for me.
I'll roll my eyes back, thinking;
I'll be the picture of flightiness today.
Assumptions will spill from my ears—
a brain storming out in furious herds;
all summer my brain will be a pasture
of tall, hissing grass, a sibilance intent on rising to character air.

Fly forgeries of z wallpaper my room: chainsaws, prop planes, wind
forcing itself through. It's a fact that the skull makes room for the brain by
talking; the brain shakes like a curse in the cranium as something dark
crawls out of my mouth. The radio is pouring weather I must knit into a
shawl. Evenings require a shawl and the wrong love, the wrong noise of
one's wrong thinking. Flies come to brain every last inkling into swarm,
into arias of amnesia and treble thoughts. No one can shoot something
that small.

I will just shoot off today; I'll just
blurt out argot in the rawest haze.
Today I'll be snoring at the kitchen table
while the radio slips into passing traffic.
I will be sworn by. I'll be clairvoyant
by keeping half in the dark. I'll know
apropos out-posts by staying home today;
by haunting my own enlarged attic
under worried clocks drum-humming
me down to make me one of their vernaculars—believe me,
black hole, you bright microscopia,
you know best how long I'll stand
stitching up grass-stained synapses
in devotion to invisible demands, whatever the invisible demands.

Miraculous Panoptic Precipitations

Rained milk and blood during the courtship
Rained fish and no flesh
Left unplundered by birds went bad
Rained tiny biting mouths
High on the hill rained feedback let it
Rained a stone from the sun which is itself
Stone lording noon
Over us rained clearest at the tail of sleep
Into a gaudy birdbath rained
Sea if sea were up there
You'd tilt your eyes at it and hiss
Counter-drag downing you
Rained Iowa in India
Changed the course of rivers
Arrows rained on bears
One person struck forgot how to read
Rained spelt round the stronghold
And mold upon the skein
Panspermia in your baffled ear once spilled
Sirens splitting night in two
Rained that you had to take bladders out of yourself
Plans for a little canoe
Spilled saliva in a goodly spot
Rained cirrus set on fire rained evaporated vaccines
Sixty god-stiff things bloated the land
What it forgot rained
Chloroform near engorged waters which made a century
Unmade raining so as not to retain
Rained to keep the told not telling
To keep pointing upward pointing
Hand come down
You're chosen to rain now rain

The Truth about Northern Lights

I'm not right. I'm interfered with
and bent as light. I tried to use the spots
for months I tried with rings.
Only now I'm thinking in cracks
that keep a modern light
lunged. I keep the porchlight on
to burn you off in ghosted purls,
the licks of which filament me.
My day-glo tongue's cutthroat.
Though I'm not clear,
I'm a sight whose star stares back;
it's a new kind of dead,
it hides its death in my cinched
testicle. That bright burr makes me
unreal and itch. By the time
I'm something else, you're making weather
with so-and-so. Everything around you
wades in queasy waves; it waits
mottled to the marrow.
My mean streak beams neon
so I won't be refracted
or led to reflections. My eyes
trick god's and kick the careless reversals
of radio cure-alls. Rays suffer
until they clench the damaged night in me:
where I go out, gone as done
in a mood as black moving through.
Darkness sits there, pleased.
An iridescent ire could not go unaired;
my limbs wicking at the window.
Look out the window.
I've outened the world
to show you real barrenness,
a void a light
warps into want and then wants
until it warps all it glances.

Night Sentence

Feathery in the corner strikes three times the fox

circulates snow hurried over white fur and I am

almost dreaming about a man in a boat if my teeth stay perfectly still

I am almost dreaming about shark teeth

on a shiny highway that escapes me into a grand scale

and is mine like a bed cracked by the ice plagues end in

that's the hole I'll dream through all that sky

snags and draws out *who*ing if I slow my breath

a candle eats air from my mouth

veining an electrical pattern I know it by the numb

and all the snow in the window is mine too in fevered grays

it makes me bright inside the moon admiring anything

could induce a stutter as if being possessed

were part of the sleeping process

to lie in the dark and see that proof is Precambrian

and snow is permission to dream of rising wet out of arctic water

my hair silver and thick as the swordfish frozen to my hand

sweating like the streetlight is also mine

it sinks the snow as birds will slow my sleep circling

a rock the ocean current surrounds in white fur

bubbling inside something bent over itself

so cold I'll almost dream the water a dead body displaces

Arctic Sun

If gold in a glimpse dim
she catches sun-coin
in her lap. She raffles off its plasma.
Until then, it sums up forgetting;
it is not a forest of suns.
If metal slants the last ray
then shucked and spent
and coming home prying
unloaded itself from her eyes.
It wants to be satisfied
and clean of satisfaction; it steals
detail because stealing makes
the hand alive. Fortune tells
the tender to sign here on the cliff.
If cashed in, cliff banks light up.
They have music you can't find
because nothing seems near enough.
If stitched in interest
if paralyzing the doorway
until the headache gets in—
breaking the window even
if inhaled then lucky:
its easy air lulls her if
that royal flash candies the view.
Its cha-ching finishes her sentences
and snaps shots of her handsome
in two coats of skin and rings
corresponding to planetary sweeps.
If outshined, if diamonding around
then the sun treasures itself until
memory haloes inside another sun
and rolls starry-eyed, its embers
breathing back. If swallowed whole
the sun relumes a sinkhole. If owed
if owed. If plenty then her hands
drip with yellow jackpots
and throw her eyes down
the sun's round mouth. If
queened, if faced, if trust
ties itself to her stake—
is is last seen.

Log Written by an Unknown Hand in the

then we plyed by guess
toward an yle hydden
where the vegetable lifee
I lead wille dye of froast
lyke a moon stuckke
in mountains that sees
& breakes our windes
in chymical wedding of sea
and far-thest governments of ayr
but I have red that daunger lye
in its voyde of light & wille
where fogge is a terryble animal
hung from the Coast
& Day is but pulse
sucked from river ironne
& the river searched
& suffered untill we anchored
by reason of sunken Rockes
which I named Queen
& a strong streame bubbling
with relics of a previous trippe
in no minutes which I called
Desire Provoketh—
weather continued thicke
& drowsiness overtook us
on the tenth day entire
then I found the sea more growne
scalles of the surface lit
by the suddenne fire of Sunne
that kerned salt on hideous rockes
(I have fathoms of like informations)
& I spotted a crag
green-granite and animalled
with no bewildering white
through a gust that harbored
a grove of firs steaming
—then we mayde use
from corpse-smell

strong as if it were insyde
my own mouthe
thus deprivation coaxed
the God lying unclaymed
to spake like a lunge on a Coast

The Sickness & the Magnet

Cursing his eyes' erasing motion
His face caught snow & his horse
Prevented falling sickness
Diadems & degrees echoed
Every red electricity spit out
He starved a beast & became full of tricks
Now a lightning maker could feel
What a lightning of metal tasted like
It hammered at him & joined disease
He felt the storm sew magnets in hems
He felt fevers of wept railings
Amazed how hot an animal is
So sorry so chattered so scat sorry so strung
Sweated horse light excruciating sweat
Birds went in & out of his mouth
He lived out of his mouth
Sucking the slap backwards
Then everything wanted to be
Killed at the rural spot

catherine imbriglio

artist's statement

I often sit with a 1939 unabridged second edition of *Webster's New International Dictionary*, a book my father—not a reader, more of a mathematician—asked for and received as a college graduation present. (His mother and father and five brothers and sisters pooled resources to give him the gift.) The editors of that dictionary fascinate me. They loved lists, of long embedded denominations—coins, dyes, grasses—of "self-explanatory" combination words—stone-asleep, stone-ground—and intricate etymological and explanatory cross-references.

I get lost in such excess, take hours to transcribe my own lists and
 interconnections.
I attend to this process as a part of my attention deficit.
Eventually this ritual is overcome by the pressures of message.
Because one also needs message to live with/in the world in one's own
 time.
The mark of each message lies in its obligation to an aural primacy.
I adhere to this primacy as a letter before proof, in an act of listening.
Here I am playing with Webster's entry under "proof," subcategorized
 under Engraving and Etching: a proof impression. (The editors
 designate one kind of impression, taken before the title or inscription
 is engraved, as "a proof before the letter.")
Starting with a dictionary entry enables me to move on and replicate this
 process of gathering, with phrasal units from books, such as George
 Johnson's *Fire in the Mind*, or stray dialogue from television.
Because when one feels oversaturated with sensory messages, it is hard to
 find an internal space from which to add anything.
Each word comes hard-earned, even to a level of reticence.
Emily Dickinson: "This is my letter to the World that never WROTE to
 Me" (my emphasis).

How would she address the question Stanley Fish asks in the beginning of
The Trouble with Principle: which is more important, giving your word,
or the person to whom you are giving your word?

To this, I imagine my father might say, "Poems don't prove anything."

Last year he gave me Webster's third unabridged, more modern, minus
1939's elaborate lists and obsessive (cf. ARTIST'S PROOF) cross-
references.

His gift makes me think a poem is an aesthetic impression that impresses
best when it is reciprocal.

Attempting poetic reciprocity (as I am doing here) may help one think
through—argue with—formulate—many such premises.

The poets whose words press upon me most—Donne, Dickinson, Stevens—
were always somehow in an argument with their worlds. (Maybe most poets
are.) Their poetry is capacious and sonic. They had unreasonable reasons for
writing it. Their interior worlds were playfully urgent and wild. From them
comes what I imagine poetry to be, the poet and the poem momentarily com-
posing themselves, managing to stay just a second ahead of what the poem lets
in as most monstrous, prodigal, raw, and alive. Reading them, you learn to
"hear" the picture. This is a condition of music (Pater by way of Ashbery) to
which I hope (having heard) all my poems will seriously, playfully aspire.

Motive

I ran away wanting you to follow and then catch up. "You" are both the viewer and the one coming down the stairs. You see her nyloned foot and then her smile. She was calling me back to the bottom of the stairs. It seemed she wanted me to rotate a responsible "if," like layering one foot over another, with no make-up on.

I don't want you to think I'm sending discretionary messages just to feed your need for compliments. When you've known someone for so long a time, the sense of politeness is stripped. The sightlines are puffy and related, like images you push, without hands, within the brain. That is to say, to see me in the flesh, you need to associate memory around a theory of "which."

At first you worried about getting set in your ways, but then you realized your problem is your ways can't get set. It seemed like each sentence had a reversible sexual drift, so that if the expression was "right out of our mouths," words could take, or be taken by, the wind. The next word was "pus"—it seemed adolescent of him.

She was looking for a synonym for the very old. The roofs and the ladders apply. The fallen petals apply. The perilous chapel applies, where something haunting about high voices filled the vaults for Michelangelo's condemned. They peered through spread fingers whose temperatures must head for the temperature of the room.

Sin she called fooling the view. At least you get some pleasure out of, a similar division of labor occurs in, dawn is no good for you. If the trees stripped, the fishermen set gill nets. Ladies and gentlemen, once again. They heard a pure voice (don't touch me, it said) with its pure way of apprehending the whole.

All along they told her "you" decide. I was having trouble discerning which was the emotional filler, the patch of river where you can pick out a piece of her distance or the woman whose words and concepts don't coincide. Against those who told me the price of meaning was going up, I argued there were words with sounds like cormorants flapping one day at a time.

Rumor

Sidestepping definitions is a normal process which is permission. She can't save them all, though the boats cutting white scars briefly into the water's body are like symbolic putdowns of the other guests. *When you finally do paint the island, paint the light so the viewer can't look at the water because of the glare in it.* She is trying to remember when the heron came to the rocks, nesting, but whose responsibility it is to speak first hampers the body's cooling mechanisms. For any definition, you need both terms, but it won't be a stable definition, as when a man calls her, pretending to be a woman. He says, Look at the ribs and the dome, the sun almost down to that building. The crib in there, giving me your measurements.

The water under the bridge at slack tide realigns the common sense system of closed forms as if it owns it. You don't own me, like the pockmarks which make a salt marsh look like your offer of a "make-up" trip. What any mark told me, I always used to believe, from the position of motion seen, as if I were the mark, until the only actual motion became what was prohibited. She's never going to ask again, having asked twice, but the change of tide will be like a rumor she'll repeat hoping it will return with something prohibitive. Once the main suspect is seen simultaneously in cities 80 miles apart, she will not get sick, though the different attitudes of wind on the surface of the salt marsh make her impersonal enough to align them with ownership.

Block Island Ferry

After the Newport Bridge, the interior of the boat is broken

by the boat's lateral roll, so this could be the horizon she wants to start
you with. At first she sees one quarter sea, then only a sliver of sea
against all-sky, but at each roll the proportion of sky and sea changes
the port window, so the imbalance makes a "has-been" out of you.
She *could* protest, as if she has willed herself to herself, but the distance
from one island to the next constitutes a learned helplessness,
like the way the loudspeaker tells her, You must
get back to the boat on time.

He held her down once, or she held him down.

By "once," I do not mean "one time only,"
only that once the water begins breaking up the sun, well, the sun,
you set the sun into blank space. You could say that it is mostly scalp,
like the scalp on the bald man who positions himself
across from the Ladies Room. If the stall doors swing open,
along with the main door, the women won't know if it is emotion
or destination sitting beside them, though either would be in motion
in relation to what the man sees inside the room. Once any motion goes
right through you, it is like your eyes trying to hold down
the sparkles breaking from the sun,

each one breaking the sequence you start with.

I Loved Ophelia

drowning done right is simply a question which doesn't hold its answer at bay, in the bay there's the mount hope bridge, the island darkens like a splinter, the sun reddens, I fire my needles, the sky wields a, let's call it a glass slipper. I'm not counting on the island coming out, a few clouds pass over: we'll get right back to you. after this message what are you so mad at? there's fennel for you. your grandma said, what smooth skin you have, too bad you aren't pretty. too bad you're so old you should have said. you should have said, I dream of mouths, mouth after mouth. of noble minds and once upon a time, too. this is how to get around everything: noble minds and once upon a time, if you believe in it. then go to sleep in my bed. last time I thought you said you were going to, I thought you said

Emily

In the photo, if I am disheveled, hanging onto the blank fence spikes,
where were your arms? There are as many different qualities in rain
as she could wish, yet we call it rain. The possibilities seem smaller as
   long
as you stay used to them. At any minute she will charge right through
me. If this is a conviction, it is one I am comfortable with.

At her grave I am caught between the two of you. Let me: for twenty-six
across the cure is a closed hand. The ice on the branches brought down tin
music. Since decisions between things are only for practical purposes,
some mornings I can keep these promises to myself such as, I do not
believe she is mouth-stopped, at never-never end.

Those promises we have difficulty with, I find. For instance, why do I hate
yellow? You were lucky, he told me, and I was. Called back, the world
comes into focus at distant intervals. First the stone slab, then the gray
hornet mask. What happens in between I have walked and guessed.
Magnetic upheavals originate deep within the sun, but because of
astigmatism my eyes are not quick. If into the dust go her private
parts, in my previous life I was blind rain.

Aubade

The dead woodchuck in the dog's mouth drooped
like a poorly tied bow. At first she couldn't get the dog
to let the woodchuck go or make the dog cross the bridge
because there were gaps between the planks.
You've probably seen this before but please don't
pay attention for the wrong reasons. A reminder
shouldn't trivialize any center or be thought of as a center,
since the sun is sidelined when it rains.

When it rains, she commits herself to the rain.
She wishes she had told her, This is not a competition
to decide who is worse off. Afterwards, on the underside
of the branches, the drops line up like teeth. That lack
of a lower jaw does not bring out the best in me. One can lie
through one's teeth, but it is only an introduction
to the laws of motion. I want to part my lips toward you,
but when the drops dry off, the empty branches are not gums.

She took twelve Beatrix Potter music boxes down from the shelf
and wound them all. The boxes delivered
tiers of music by striking apostolic tongues.
She couldn't distinguish any melody until the hedgehog
dressed as a washerwoman played longer than the rest.
Then she heard "O what a beautiful morning." To understand
the song she internalized it, but behind the song she sensed
something prehistoric which wants like this.
It would have to kill the song.

Museum

Where she sits, there is only a partial view of the courtyard,
which seems to be three stories of dead space, though they've
placed yellow flowers to define the borders on each side.
If I give this to you, you'll have
to keep it by drawing the eye imperfectly up,
through the groundfloor arches to the orange nasturtiums
which fall from the balconies because
it is April there. The space is structured by
means of the relationship of the arches to the eye. Her story
is, the tiniest moment matters in the foreground, so she stays
in the distance where the perspective is influenced
by looking at the gothic through a roman eye.
If she touched the carvings on the arches indiscriminately,
the salts and oils on her fingers would wear down the figures
in her eye. The courtyard is an area of enforced immobility,
with imported statues, which she should be hardened to by now.
She can see only one of the statues. The passersby talk,
but if she doesn't listen carefully she can make their voices
into a saxophone's hum. How do you
get to those things I don't know names for,
as if everything which supported a structure
took sides? You're supposed to want to go back. Even if I agree
each story has to be artificially stopped, you could
draw me into a space between the arches,
into the iconoclasm of each breath taken there.

Say for me.

Say forth, say forthwith, in the name of colors, of real colors, in the name of real colors named, in the initial real color named, say Brunelleschi, say curvature, say Sir Francis Crick. For what we are about to receive, not only show all fragile passengers, red in the initial appearance of a material surface, say this is the place, this is the effort on our part, this is where we'd say, "This is." To expend our dream hoard that the years ago came from the ancient monotreme lane, enter "the lovely ropemaker," 1520–1566. In memory processing, in egg laying, in "let them alone so they'll come home," from to look at, add species hours, add breath toll, add an REM script. To the inquiring name, recognizing it needed room, it needed feet, for somewhat as though, it, you, drew, birdscatterer, through the engine of, the stem of, from up to your body breakable, i.e., "if all the trees were one tree." It drew through its tongue, its backwater, its layer upon layer, its layer upon layer beneath the larger layer, for when in your shock upon shock, in the name you were named, be monkfish, be milkwort, be mate.

Psalm

I.

Each now dropped

Lay your hands upon me, you in the black bent grass, the body in motion
that stays in motion, so too in your drifting to or from me, in the pictures
of the body that provoke the body, *judica me*, you in the blackpoll warbler,
judica me, you in the black-tailed godwit. It wasn't on purpose was it, in
the way you get it down or keep it down, my texture to your texture, in the
body as motion that stays as motion, *judica me*, which one of us, like spit.
One of us should try breathing in the mirror, each mirror holding yet
another mirror, it *was* something like communication wasn't it, how many
persons to a copper or silver goblet, how many persons from holding out
their bowls. So too you in this drifting to or from me, in the pictures of the
body that provoke the body, let me not from the circulation of
impediments, let me not from accommodation to the pose.

II.

No internally fixed order of stages stop. Under incremental light
conditions stop. I look out and see under the lilacs stop. From woodbine
to woodbine stop. Day unto day one tree frog two duckboards three goat
moths stop. Made you look made you look made you look you stop. Were
word of godetia real word stop. If without if without finding stop. What
impudicity what who me stop. There is stop no speech no language where
the voice from the wilderness stop. When it comes a'courtin' and we all go
stop. Yours to then yours to wend watch stop. Day unto day while we take
its sweet time stop all rise.

III.

Spiny wings that, suppose that

Break their teeth with your lips, break the teeth of the dumb flowers, open
wide the calyx, for when you do what you do, I who you your honor, broke
out in teeth, the alleged teeth, for at just that time, admit, for open wide,
admit, were you or were you not, *selah*, down beside me among the cow
wheats, the bull thistles. Go for the throat. Now we see it, now we, in sun
mouth, in ripened seed head, casual, seriatim, party of the first part wreak
party of the second. Rattle the big pharmaceuticals. Reign in with limit

list. Rattle for rattle, rattle *of* rattle, constrained by, gag ordered, most wanted, grift. So moved. Hoop ash, basket ash, a set of promises, a mimicry. And then, an if then, a nothing to me. I lost my place. Partings of the first part beneath a parting of the second. So moved. Ballast love, when a rain coursing through me. Here. Hearsay. In here you'd say.

Gospel According to the Middle

I.

In the beginning was the who, and the world was with who, and the world was who. The beginning was both before and after the who, and because of the beginning, the world could light-hearken, light-hearken to all that it was, to all that could be made. I am not the who but the one who comes across the who. I am the one who separates the singer from these strains. Between us was the string and the lute was with string and the lute was string. And all things come from strings, begotten not made. They were in the middle, not made. Her eccentricity was, on the other hand, made. I have seen it missing, the lute, the middle of the lute, who from the beginning was the one from whom all things were made. From the beginning, the lute was also an if, the one who was with the if, and the one who was if, begotten not made. If the water could be clear, it could be green and scummy, if the water was clear or green and scummy, it was not the lute, it was not the middle of the lute, because in the beginning the lute was an if, and from the beginning, water, yea the water, it could be made.

I say unto you lute, I say unto you light-hearken, I say unto you whom I do not say. She was with me and she was me. It is no longer the beginning. It is the middle and the middle is cruel. I say unto you, through you and in you and with you, you who join with me separately or come together maybe towards dusk, or maybe much earlier, light-heartened, before we go swimming. It is always useful to go back and say you are merely towards dusk, or would have come much earlier, since even before you are after, and before-after is the middle, is the middle where you may be saying, who was that if so light-hardened in its distributions to the brain.

II.

"Whereas, once upon a time, I walked along the white cliffs, for miles and miles, getting white chalk on my shoes. When a man hailed me from the brush about 20 yards above, I realized how stupid I was for walking alone. Sometimes I think that in a concurrent life he must have done me in, because even now when I think of it, my feet sweat so as to eventually ruin my shoes."

reception reception money loaves fishes owl rockband children's stories
reception reception
reception reception money loaves fishes owl rockband children's stories
reception reception

claim claim reception reception money loaves fishes owl rockband
children's stories claim claim reception reception
claim claim reception reception money loaves fishes owl rockband
children's stories claim claim reception reception

reception reception claim claim reception reception claim claim
reception reception claim claim reception reception

III.

Topographical shapes

Irregular masses of gray matter

It is the spirit that gives life, the flesh is useless. This is called begging the
blessing. This is called who is kissing who knew. At the asses' bridge
(pons asinorum), some basic tests for the inexperienced mathematician.
The soft mute, the middle mute, where reason is transacted. Let all
numbers be in the set voice, the intermediate voice, between the active
and the passive. Let who is kissing who knew. For heightened a little, the
lights are combative. You, sit with your pants down until I tell you you can
move. The anchorman, citing military wisdom, warns against fighting the
"last war," i.e., the previous war, not the one that will end with the earth's
extinction. Please stand. Please be seated. Soon I will no longer be
speaking to you in figures. The soft mute, the middle mute, where reason
is transactive. Let if the spirit give life, the flesh be useless. Let if one
brood nest and one brood nest then two. This is called begging the
blessing. This is called who is kissing who knew. In a little while and then
in a little while. Money loaves fishes reception reception. Money loaves
fishes reception who.

Gospel According to One
Who Always Needs an Audience

She gives it to herself

He gives it to himself

Supposing him at first to be the gardener, half of his plants on one side, half on the other, he taught me how to measure rows with right measure, that the garden was always a garden, meaning, a gamble, back-strength and arm-strength on one side, the elements and wildlife on the other; he used to plow in the mornings, take produce to his wife and all the neighbors in the late afternoons—early evenings; like his brothers and sisters, he was what we used to call bull-headed, not as with his music moderato, as if from dusk to dusk he could win the fields, win at the law of averages; for years, hoe in hand, he managed the weed crawlers and the stink grass, but even so, supposing him at first to be the gardener, I was wrong: when he got old the garden was no longer a garden, meaning, a gesture; so as, I say to you, dusk to dusk, nothing is as it was when he first appeared.

Please stand. Please be seated.

Gospel according to what rises to our consciousness.
Gospel according to temper temper temper tune.
Gospel according to some man's stolen wallet.
Gospel according to how he cleared the room.
Gospel according to false cohosh = the blue cohosh, of Algonquian origin.
Gospel according to how we stand our moods.
Gospel according to y while x is happening.
Gospel according to the sun according to the moon.

Gospel According to How We Throw Stones

Q. *Can one recognize a dream as comic? I mean from inside the dream interpret an image and laugh? Aunt and uncle trying to keep you from leaving by shouting "poison sumac, poison sumac in your path"?*

A. Those who are well have no need of a physician. Through leaching, mother and daughter elements can be swept away. They read the text and predict it will happen. Fifteen young women die in a fire because they aren't properly veiled. Start talking. Don't pass it over. Grapestone, backstone, goatstone, hairstone, milkstone, bird stone, stone root, stone clover. The fault lies not with our scars but with our narratives. Let us play. Let us play out. Pins and needles. A patch of new cloth on an old cloth. Surgery will be done as an outpatient procedure. You sew and sew. Dehiscence. Septicidal. Do you hear me. Do you hear me now.

Q. *So if it's only your dream followed by my dream, of separate cities, separate reconciliations, do you know (and if you do, how do you) are we actually harnessing the stone's throw?*

A. My great uncle sold crushed stone to the city of Fall River which used it to build roads. Whereas "myth does not provide a blueprint for pragmatic political action" (Armstrong). Monsters will be monsters, see me boiling each liquid by dropping in hot stones. Granite for granite, sledgehammered, split (saxifrage grows in stony places): what you know and do not know (the world as weighted weight) is smashable (use grievance grown from grief, as from a foundation of crushed stones). But what if in dreams we're held responsible, hold out your hand, it's nearly night now—for you, here's honey yellow, also known as honey middle stone.

JOANNA KLINK

ARTIST'S STATEMENT

In poems I am trying to find my bearings through a world that at times feels remote and inchoate and struck blank with noise. I would like to place myself in a field of deep attention, and out of that attention come to feel and regard with more acute understanding what is there. I write to be less hopelessly myself, to sense something more expansive than where I speak from. This at least is my hope. If I could do this in language, I would cross over into a world where isolation falls away and separateness is eased, where there is no need to be numb in order to get by—and every silence is instructive, every perception part of a widening movement of voice and light and air, so that it is possible to be fully there, it is possible to feel the very shape of change. Wallace Stevens stepped out onto the blue-gray beach he dreamed in his head. He found a way to walk there, in the presence of quieting patterns, despite the very basic, broken loneliness that stays with you in your dreams. Elizabeth Bishop fought off a great, shapeless darkness by concentrating her attention on quartz grains and crumbs and weathered wood, the subtle perceptual folds of experience that might be backed by a light unavailable even to her eyes. Her patience and discretion held her to the world. And T. S. Eliot, despite his terror of other people, made his poems into expansive, ritual spaces, cathedrals of dusk and inwardness where he could feel grief among others and could stay, a little while, in their presence. These poets *thought* in their poems. They could not separate physical pain from its mental shape, or physical joy from the freedom of wandering far within an idea. In their poems they struggled always to reassemble themselves, to locate those floating, invisible powers that might hold them together, hold them to a place. And they did this through language that was "unnatural," far from ordinary speech and its hallmark directness, because they were wary of speech that simplifies our experience and so corrodes our experience. I don't have the words to do what is required. If I could, I would, as John Berger has written, "[defy] the space that separates."

Orpheus. Eurydice. Hermes

"How is it with you, that you do bend your eye on vacancy, and with the incorporeal air hold discourse?"

I.

Huge birds flap through the toxin dark.
She would prefer it on the whole if he spoke in a whisper.
In the air, feet floating over the smooth porphyry path,
Orpheus in a blue wool coat, Eurydice shaking.
Hermes flits between them.
If he were more inclined to speak he would say it works
first upon sensation would say it shimmers
through the natural arcades and alleys of the body
would say then leaks slowly back into fact.
God of this and god of that with beating wings at his ankle joints.
Huge birds murmur in the scrawny pines.
Her hair films with ice then hardens into sticks.
Bits of zero paper up her throat.
The sound so weak it hardly reached his ears.

II.

Eurydice there's been talk—
I am supposed to look straight ahead.
Eurydice take my hand.
I have been instructed to look straight ahead.
Are you hurt?
When you say today you mean—
This bridge, this bedroom.
I would prefer it on the whole if you spoke in a whisper.
Have you—
I have, yes. I think so, yes.
Are you saying
I am saying it.
. . . It's been one continuous accident—
—What did you say?
I think it's lovely the color of it.

III.

Hermes likes things to come easily. He didn't ask for this job.
He pulls the hood over his shining eyes. Technically,
if you count the business about the stolen cattle, God of Herdsmen
and Fertility of Herds, God of Luck, Furtiveness and Trickery,
Patron of Oratory with a General Interest in Literature
(some ghosts congregate by the brink) God of Roads
and Boundaries, Sleep and Dreams, God of Faring and The Distant
Message (their shuffling drops down the gorge, half-mile below
a fish leaps) Patron of Travelers and Rogues Vagabonds and Thieves,
Patron of Gymnasts . . . They move across a windless meadow.
Bright unshaken place. Hurry.

IV.

He forgets that he can't—he forgets the condition.
He forgets himself.
He forgets her.
He wants assurance she is still there.
He is afraid she might disappear again.
After all she was suddenly gone.
He thinks she may be blushing.
He would like to address her.
He would like to touch her small shoulder bone.
This is a generation before Troy.
His feet hurt his head burns. He is concerned,
undisciplined, seeks recognition—she is a room full of paintings—
As her foot drags behind him bits of star chip off the iron rock.
And they are going unnoticed—nothing but the unresisting air—
Hermes herds them forward, touching her on the temple, pushing
flat against his back. Ceaseless prologue, return him
more violently, there is no ordinary life, perception is
thirsty. In the claustral dark, bracken grind against their legs.

V.

I can think of three ways in which an accident might happen.
(Eurydice opens her mouth and suggests)
You were exasperated with what you had done. You were impatient.
You were absent-minded—your attention was wandering.
(He lowers his eyes) It's a technical problem.

(Hermes growls It's not a technical problem)
Do you realize
It does
For example
O but they wilt like other things.
After all I'm behind you.
On condition—
On condition Sir I'm behind you.
(Sir, Angel of the Upper Air, Unnatural Officer, Minister of What
Keeps, Illustrious Bishop, Jewel of Clerics, Floating Mirror of the Church)
(Whatever brings it up into the nervous system more suddenly)
(Whatever nails the salt-flesh onto the bed.)

VI.

Would this be pointless for you.
I think probably.
You prefer to be alone?
I like the impersonality of it.
Is this because the memory is more interesting or because the presence is
disturbing?—You've stopped. Have you stopped?
(Love anywhere but in me!)
Does this irritate you?
(Anywhere but in me take this.)
If I could play for you now (Cries Hermes O play for us now)
Don't be silly even Tantalus has not gone back to his waves.
Is this not . . .? (Proceed heavenward)
(Shudders her bone-colored skin)
You practice injury. You comment on the thing you love.
Sometimes I hardly know what I am doing, sometimes it disappears
    completely.
Of course you lose the damaged forms more easily in darkness.
(Reaches his arm back) (Into the robber speech)

VII.

Do you feel it when I take hold of your hand?
Hermes, they are becoming free-concordance of nerves
along the walking spine, her soft-clipped leg
leaning into the freakish outline
(Sisyphus sits on his rock to listen)

(For example the snow understands the orchard as it buries it)
Do you feel it when I take hold of your hand?
(Frost burns in bits between her shoulder bones)
She would prefer it on the whole if he spoke in a whisper
(his voice dry) (does she feel it)
Something cracking there are bridges over voids—
When I take hold of your hand
(Up ahead a ray of natural optic light)
(Whose feet, whose bodies do they wear)
Hermes semaphores wildly in the dark.
Zero of the bone.
Then her wide soul squints and the thought
grafts easily onto the animal air.

Scarcity

Brush of sunlight on the dry grass.
Thrum of a bird against wood
and the long minute after.
Not in fits and starts

as they began it. And the space
between them in which they are held—
is hidden, is important—here,
here you are, in each way

beautiful—I couldn't stay an hour longer.
Little song from the tree,
bring what you can I will take it.
In the hours that follow we may be

increased—to feel that
place in the head. The hours
issue into words. Into words we say
street, into children crossing say

here is a morning and
evidence of bird but no bird.
When it comes to pull us apart
stay familiar. Stay outside the realm

of what could be said here—the grass
burnt, delicate, a light on my hands.
And a street across which
you are speaking to me, sadly,

like a question, gathering
nerves. Today is specific—
a portion of love or sorrow.
Is specific—shadows rest on a field,

noon-quiet, rain muttering the street.
Say *today*, say *okay*, say *protect*
what you can—is missing, is important—
mountain blown under grass, outcrop

of the shadows the children outside
the realm of what could be said
here in fits and starts guessing
protesting these days when they hurt

but for the places I'd reach you,
rain-blurred on the steps—and the small
meannesses disguised as freedoms—
in each way my poorness in this world.

Sea by Dusk

Comes to gather you from clocks and says *be moon*,
be progress. Gathers the bitter fact of chance and says
change in every way. Depending on the harvest,

a sadness glassed in autumn, depending on the sea.
Shatters the lullaby, lush and drugged, that would settle
in the downcast reaches. *You who bear the light in you*

bear the deep compass, unending corrosion,
an irreparable white meadow. Gather what voyage you can,
a sound far into water, susurrous in the array of salt

and drifting sunlight, *what is left for us to live*. Below water
or close above, rhythms emptied in the flutter of Pacific,
without limit, a human sound breaking hard against this air,

endure, says *become what you can* in the summer fluency of waves.
Sleep, saline, gathers the currents of blue driftwood,
says a hymnal loose with eiderdown and light—

and comes to prize you in the hour of your late undertaking,
your new and precise fear. Listen, lean, that you might feel,
in the warm blurring of waves, the opening and closing of flowers,

a circadian call that pulls all desolation toward clearing,
be ready, *be shirred*, task of light, a cadence of star
and constancy, *change*, dropping far in pressured water,

sails of shadow *change in every way*. As in the halls of night
the swallows gather up whole acres of past error,
vision into vision, printed in the last coral light spilled out

across the tides, your arms, gathered and withstood
in such arcades of stars and sleeping fish, within, without,
pulling near—do I know you—issued in calligraphies of brine

on darkness, *turn*, *return*. We are drifting out of phase,
lost, calendar-sprung, and feel the wings slanting through air
above these fleeting museums of the sea, held

within a single note that moves in pain, pattern, scarcity
and abundance, *abide*, *turn and return*, some small, far happiness—
and the nocturne grows within each drowsy marine creature,

rope, tack, slowing muscle of the heart, depending on the tides,
depending on the air, a perfect mammal stillness
beneath all flights of caution, the net cast far into

space, *who*, clock, stopclock, falling lace, beautiful and slow
across the warming skin, in the slipping borders, your body,
shall be safe, unscheduled beyond the sea-torn cemetery,

gracious fields, the gardens, as in a true response
to daylight, here, unearthed in cooling water,
full of suffering, mirrors, moving countries

of fish and floating grass, your hopes, receding
terror, recognize you, it says, no loneliness, no more
loneliness, *open*, it says, *your arms.*

Circadian

Dividing time equally between earths, there in the coldness
pulling south, blue-flooding dusk, a few stars.
You are irreducible, there where you stand,
and all the mountains dropping into water.
To what else would you give such care?
Each thing made in the moment we hear.
I understand when the winds rinse ice across the mountains
and the mountains throw out their rock and burden, and the light
and the feel of the light are the beginning of what we know.
How close can you come?
Come into the world again.
Birds are moving through sky.
One may be flying below roof-level—
it rises when there are breezes.
One night and division sets in, two and we wonder
what pardon, three and you are sleeping poorly.
Simplicity remembering there never was a time.
There never was a time a time prefacing spacious disquiet.
There never was a below sea-level where the bird
flew warmly in water. There never were stars
bobbing on the surface or stars sinking.
The fish dream as the stars fall past them.
The bird seeks a place to land and cannot, in the swell of tides,
in the shallow sandstops, find it. All freedoms
drawing us toward. The flocks of geese
swim in the light-flecked night, and bring stories of arrival.

River in Dusk

What wind there was
What light there was was not
enough, I could not
hear beyond a cry a signal
beautiful idea to touch
you or wince where
faint against the glass you
sensed my hand—darkness
icy with bells—how
in the answer we felt
a sweeping diminishment
of things, fleets
of noise, faraway
wash of sequoias, and separate, clouded,
flat, haunting, and haunting
the surfaces bent in river
air against the clear
afternoon
Who told you *time will come*
Who finally seized the wind figure
dragging aqueous regions inside
And inside the warrant
And inside the indifference through which
you are invited to pass, what
would occur in the half-
second of your leaning to
speak me that music
(Isn't it better to *live*)
You are right here
You are part of my persuasion

Shooting Star

Nova, pure periphery, glassed into the immobile black, a few light
dispatches from abroad, streaks of glass trailing white in the
   commonplace
hour, autonomous, available in the beds of stars and interrupted councils,
argument of the untended topiary, their animals rising in shapes
   unintended
to move, though we suffer distinction, and at the hand of the shadow-
   marvels
the promontories sail, and still mistake the morning's garden-
   immobility,
birches once fluent with yellow light, that what was sent here is altered,
what was witnessed casual, terraced into the available, shapes of love
or maybe only shapes in the bed, single star streaking in cracked silence
above our argument, casual, intended to move, intended to harbor light,
though we hurt each other, and failing this witness mistake fluency,
some cry obscured in the bed beneath my answer, bearing the old
   autonomies,
to interrupt our sky's night-flying council which, threaded and glittering,
could make us, in the sudden prescription of that dropping line of
light, still, or simply quiet, and cease in time to be ourselves.

Lodestar

A lodestar held lightly in the sky above a gray
page of snow. Someone speaks a word
and the boats are born to time, trailing out against the ice.
And we judge this valuable—weather undone across a field,
the boats soft black discs upon the whitening water.
And the heat that forms within our throats
as we stand and look out. Who are you, next to me?
To shine in unawareness like the ice at night on the field.
To say the only thing you want—boats below a lodestar,
and in another country, beyond a gray wave of snow.
Late afternoon in our eyes, and somewhere a girl
sitting in a chair, emerging from thought or
preparing a future. Seeds float through the air
beneath a fire maple—it is late in the day or it is
autumn. Someone brings me a newspaper
—it is you. Had I understood what portions
would be lost or made solid by the pressures of such
emptiness. The lodestar rises each evening in winter,
mute in its ripping distance, and the fire maple
drops a few leaves in the casual winds. Farther out,
someone says a word into the summer air
and a bird emerges from the lawn's warm shadow,
a deep gray spread across the northern sea
where boats form a slow nomenclature of movement,
and everywhere we look out upon a darkness whose scarcity
we cannot comprehend. You are always nearby
and I turn to you or touch you. And in the ports already
the shipbuilding has begun, men tugging at steel
through the clear blows of metal.
We watch them as though through water,
involved as we are in the unaccomplished,
and a cold film of ocean is swept into sky—
seagulls resting against the liquid light, the fringe
of a crowd drawn, like us, to stare midway into sea,
into a field I have tried for so long to pull
free from. How remote the months between us,
the slight glow of our bodies in these rooms, a few words
that hold their sound across the stillness of hours.

You feel a star in its private heat above a field,
a woman curled into sleep or walking among the long
bars of shadow-trees through which pour shining
coins. To each belong the corrections of light,
the suffering that shall not heal, the singing that lifts
—washed, unwinged—from a small boat at sea.

malinda markham

artist's statement

As a child, I firmly believed in ghosts. Only a slender seam separated the this-world of playground sounds and schoolwork and an other-world of images, imagination, and silence. Of the two, the latter intrigued me more, ruled as it was by suggestion and unexpectedness. Children hungrily take the world in and grant each piece equal weight. I try to keep a similar sense of immediacy and actuality when I write. Rilke believed that the only criterion for art is necessity. My poems are driven by language and its sounds, but behind them is always a sense of reaching, a need to reach. Usually, the poems grasp for a sense of memory or a scrap of history. I instinctually write in search of chronological, logical, linguistic connections that cannot ever be fully present. Every ghost would tell a story, but it wouldn't tell it well.

When I write, in some ways, I'm obsessed by questions of truth, even though we can't speak of essentialism anymore. Even though I wouldn't. However, I write with a directed, quiet but voracious curiosity, and curiosity needs an object. I'm not curious about meaningless or emptiness; I need to know what that empty-looking space tastes like and what meaningless might sound like if we sat very still and waited. The body is important to me as a sensing machine, but I try to ask my poems to be small bodies of their own. In my first book, *Ninety-five Nights of Listening*, I hoped to make each poem its own world, with linguistic reverberations that would connect that world to the rest. One poem in the book ends, "Birds / freeze in the sky. We pluck them, / small berries, not knowing / otherwise / how to remember the scene." Any small bit of sensory material might suggest a whole, and if birds elide into berries, then . . . they actually do. I work in metaphors; I think in metaphors. If an accidental simile slips into a draft, I usually remove it by the end.

Since I've lived in Japan for the last three years, one of my greatest influences has been distance—physical and cultural distances, plus the distance between the two languages and that between what we intend to say and how it is received. Before I moved to Japan, though, the intimate distance of folk- and fairy tales (from both Japan and Europe) fascinated me and became the starting point for a series of poems. More recently, I've been engaging with *ukiyo-e,* especially work by Kawanabe Kyosai and his daughter, Kyosui, whose paintings look, to an untrained eye (mine), exactly like his. I'm very interested in buried narratives, stories that rise close to the surface but never waver there for long. And I'm interested in the sensory details that overtake and reshape the small histories, that insist on a different way of marking, measuring, and arranging time. In my work, memory has failed, but vestiges of it remain, and the distance between what is recalled and what forgotten keeps me writing on.

The Rock in the Garden Allows People In

When the wind blows the air inside
Shimmers like wire. Any staircase

Winds to a wall. Drops of rain
Are watery coins so who can really complain

Trees fill with birds that tuck
Themselves in like fruit. You know

The rain will fall, first north and then
South the ground

Will furl and sigh if you see a stick
Figure out past the spine

Of the fence call out something
A name. The ground there is shattered

With twigs and all wood you see
Can only catch feathers like fire

To Understand Flight

Wet hands work quickly, cartilage shines into light.
No need to repeat what you've seen

Of me, but yes I would anchor this house
To the ground if I could. One day,

The grass said to the rain, *Do not leave.*
Outside this house of memory and bricks, I plucked

A wing to see the mechanics of flight. How could
Anyone have moved with another's skin

Exposed like this and waiting? Don't think that the pull
Didn't hurt or the sound. I feared the sky

Ready to answer in rain. To loosen feathers,
first close the eyes to spare them.

That day, gray light spilled into crevices,
Covered my hands in down. I was warm.

After Aesop

An animal lives under the water. Hear children
calling out the window like glass.

Water in the hand roars like the sea and orders itself into pleats.
I am thirsty, thinks the bird. Who

could possibly resist?

Whatever moves draws nearby objects into its shape. Come with me
once, I will make you into

whatever you please.

This is a cage, a desert, a fear.

They string balconies with nets to keep the pigeons out. Over garbage to
   keep out the crows.
There are two ways to devise this world. In one,
I nail nets to the posts; in the other, I watch a net keep me

from food. This is a plum, a bone, an excuse.

In sleep, I wait beneath the webbing to see if anyone
tries to take me despite.

This world is noisy in squares.

I am thirsty, said the painting on the wall. Water is drawn like a lament
between two blue hills and the museum

that's closing. Wings bruise the glass. Already a bird has swallowed

the paint and its master.

"Come again," the sign says.
Don't speak. Push bills through the slot in the door.

Where is the cage now, when animals swim without moving? Bring the
   mouth to water—
What memory do you touch?

What water? Originally, the character for *grief* was drawn partly with *mind*,
partly with *upturned foot*. In the dictionary, it's

Entered between *tempt* and *to melt*.

Just look this time.

The hotel is open, if anyone wants rest. Money in the basin and weather in the palm. This is not sky, not water.

To drink.

With a tearing of wings, the bird threw itself into the frame.
Nets opened and closed, looking

Remarkably like hands. Comfort, anyway, lives in the eyes,
not the mouth. A passer-by

Will arrive to abbreviate the scene.

#301 A pigeon, driven by thirst, saw a basin [*krater*] of water in a painting and believed it to be real. So, with a great flapping of wings, the bird hurtled itself against the picture rashly and broke the tips of its wings. Falling to the ground, the pigeon was caught by a stranger who happened to be there. (Aesop 223)

Obedience / Intention to Hunt

Swing the bird over the brook. Snap the hood off and sing
your own safety. Sing mine. I have eaten off the ground
and am harder for it. How many feathers are necessary
for flight? I balance on a branch and examine the twigs.
Can you see the air, how far it is from here? You only a speck,
the crowd a quick inhalation of wind. With careful arms,
I will not fall. To capture each bird like anything lost.

Hard nights snap at the waistcoat for warmth. All tunnels
are gentle, and water is cold. How much more
could I offer? For a handful of grains, I would give you
the sky on a leash, circled and quick. Could a thread
stretch from your hand to the sun? The eye is sharp,
and the will only falters. Already I could test half
your theories of flight. From this branch, the world startles
into wings. Your mouth is open in what appears
to be joy. I spoke one name through this. Did you hear?
Just hold the bird steady, think medicinal thoughts.

Petition

Feed the sparrows, and they will feed you
in turn. Love the enemy, his buttons are bright.
Fever rises like lies, it settles in a pocket
that begs to be touched. Can you discern
which arrows are mine? I speak the same
as anyone here. The house was built of sticks and wool.
When ceiling beams moved at night,
we swaddled them with silk. When cracks in the eaves
closed, pigeons moved to the sills and startled
into glass. Serve tea to the guests and fold
their linen in swans. Fruit fills
their mouths, little spoons. Let violins lull
the ears shut. Let marrow break between the teeth
in warmth. When the sky curves in its own wet path,
I will name all that I know. When calling-sounds
left like water, in stains, I set acorns on fire
and floated them down the river for luck. All this
is yours for the asking. On the day I am narrow as glass,
you be the sun do not let me grow cold.

The Orange Tree Glistens

From all the others I accept these gifts, but from your mouth I absolutely refuse one—Aesop #122

Speak in the voice of defense. The boar ran, I pulled a knife. (this is plum) Grass grew in tufts about the throat, and I tried to speak. The water darkened in pitch. (hard root) Cranes do not bury their cries in the ground. So run, the man said. Swallow once and then go. Spare the paper door the fire. Cotton the wound to shield the blow. I can sleep in this place. (hardy stock) We were together. Words raced from the gravel right into his mouth. I swam. I gave him fruit that was nothing like me. (apricot cold and rare and good) Strew your fine skirts, and who will remember you here? Burning ground doesn't speak. I cannot touch you like this, split on a plate. Enter the stories: The crow spoke in the struck voice of men. I dropped to my knees. This is bounty. (this is) A skinned kind of guilt.

Having Cut the Sparrow's Heart

1.

Named for a color, I slept in your pocket.
All the first day,

It rained. Concealed as a flower,
I thought, Why not a flower?

The body divisible, closing at night.

In the morning, to hear
Sighs of the hunt. I swallowed

Animal fear. We conversed as one
Blade of grass

To another. Bright stories shone
In your mouth

& still do.

2.

The queen eats the doves
That perch on her sill. Names

Each to each to make the deed
Harder. A round

Locked room. Spiders nest. I am
Your best wish,

A collection of sounds
You spoke once

Out of fear. You were young.
When the bird

Is plucked, I cut butter
Into broth and line the platter

With green. The stars are so many
Stones I fear

Will be falling. In sleep
You almost brush

My hair with your hand.
I don't mind.

We Folded the Hours and Set Them in the Rain

Water fills the balconies. People wave from the window, flower tops drown and are useless. We set the town on its side, drained the bricks and penciled in mortar. Penciled in people, whose limbs washed away or their mouths. Please, she said, stop speaking. The phone line snaps with the plum weight of birds. Sometimes eyes focus on light. The mouth is all and fills my legs with cotton. Rain-filled streets look convincingly like milk. We made a town of sticks and arranged ourselves in it. I sewed the lawns stem by stem and breathed on them lightly. Birds fly if you blow from one direction, then let them alone.

We folded the rain when it pelted our skin. We slipped on stones. Our limbs are ships and float like leaves. When did I break into offerings like this? Houses swell in flood, colors run into the lawns. I remember the feel of a person beneath me. I remember stairs under my feet. I walked without crushing the trees. Put words into a machine and tell me who is speaking. Hours swell into statues. They cover their eyes. Once we built a paper town, wire chimneys caught on the sky. When it rained, whole streets disappeared and the people. I couldn't lean gently enough when I moved.

Compendium Notes

To cut an animal tongue, to turn the body
to gold. Figure burst whole from fruit,
then bent back in. Your skin is fresh,
the bruise is just a moment and fine. The man,
his hand sink into the sea. A woman on another,
a knife at her eye. There are stories. To swell
(a mother), to retract into figurative sleep.
Embed a word in a single rib & live
eighty years longer than the rest. Tie cloth
around the eyes. A body covered in blue
will be safe, the eyes turn up on cue. What is severed,
what is kneeling, what prostrate on the ground.
Unveil the legs in monstrous glee. This is not
a feast and at least one lack cannot
be avenged. Fallen persimmons quiet the eyes.
What climbs, what steals, what severs
in threes. One opening leads to the next.
This is only my mouth, I'm sure you know
the rest. To break, to turn to liquid, to drink
the answer down. I for one have given. "Send
the butcher back when he arrives at the gate."
A paper bird melts in the rain. Its rider stares
death in the mouth and can't speak. A figure of light,
a lie, a woman so pure children only believe.
To sow, to steep, to follow unthinking. Animal
love a tree too much. Be killed by what it has planted.

Of Children on Wood

fire blows left of the outstretched
tongue here is a knife
a gesture
near the chin

fingers cocked the bird
held straight from the chest
a mourning device

sing boy this is your moment
your mouth fit to choose

something helpful
a name

do you know how it feels
to pull hair like a sibling

to break the bird to spare
its awful speech this is

relapse another intrusion
a day to sing a hole

in the ground
sister on the roof weapon
near her face

a shovel to pray
for something like proof
they do adult things
with no words

to describe them this
is the mercy
of children the world almost

untouched it curls
around shoulders (any)
grateful to hold them

mark mcmorris

artist's statement

Entrepôt

If we walk in language as on the bottom of an ocean that has been emptied out, where the water was is the echo of a geological epoch, the echo of ships breaking apart in a gale. I wanted to disrupt the logic of the propositional sentence, Rosmarie said. The structure that asserts identity, that proposes, my example, black is black. Let each man do what he is made for and all will be well, Renan and Plato said. I am made to lift agricultural equipment, I said, to hitch mule to awkward plough and to boilerhouse. Let me also say—although I cannot guarantee my allegiance to any poetics beyond the ongoing and temporal activity of writing it out—let me say that I think of poetry as a dialogic form, as a rendezvous and entrepôt, the null space of burglary where strange things congregate and begin to speak in dialects prohibited in either full day or full darkness, as a sonic field construed for the meeting of many vectors of light some of which are dark since they dream of anticolonial utopias, chance meetings after the society of surrealists has folded up the banner and the order of image and me me me me and the technicians of signs have returned from the wilderness to ordinary language games—

> For all inwreathed
> This imagined music
> Traces the particular line
> Of lines meeting
> > by chance or design
> > (Zukofsky)

—only to find again that the large aircraft carrier has inviolate propellers though maybe a newer name, nevertheless, like a spinnaker of light that passes through an immigration checkpoint in New York, I must continue to make sense even if I grow small as the battleship nears the horizon of its desire after which my voice and my body will fall out of the picture and hold to the virtue of hearing and trying not to stint, in the American grain, immigrant with another dialect in my mouth, with the body at one tethering site and the mind both here and there, and taking into account the nonidentity of a social subject with any private account of a self (polyphonous, discordant, conflicted, diachronic), seeing that I must use your speech and that you have already decided upon how things are and that I am black, and in return I will make a different possible interlocutor within the poem and between the poem and whatever approaches to look for it, in the public parks, as the tongue changes, adds another twist to the "twisted path of struggle" (Bakhtin) known as the English language, in the understanding that to play a game where one learns the rules as the game unfolds can have the advantage of firing synapses that had grown rusty with the damp air of a logorrheic society devoted to having more cotton, more highways, more poverty, more Negroes, more inane system leaders, more gated golfer precincts, more of the same poem, more one-stop-shopping for ideas, more guns, more underclass dying daily, more empire, more amnesia of murderous psychosis, more and faster connections to more banks and deceitful doggerel ministers, can at least decry monopoly and official ideal happiness and practice freedom to go astray, to be in a state of errancy, call it stitching a coat of many colors that unstitches subjectivity and that no patriarch would be seen in, least of all the captain of an aircraft carrier or a media mogul, or call it a way that local and oral, song talk to sing (Singh), can cohabit with creaking and croaking, "I did not know how to make the pebble sing," the poet wrote (Brathwaite), call it "to imagine a language is to imagine a form of life" (Wittgenstein) where the current form has no currency that the mind can use to fend off oblivion, hearing what the older poets said like Blake or like Keats said of the forms of life they knew and to hate it is a virtue, they said to me one evening, to be an iconoclast will land you in church but at least you can write poems if not smash the system, so go ahead and be disobedient, end all talk of infiltration fouling circuitry disjunctive syntax contamination and become a ghost in the machine or join an underground river or not join, and see where categories crack open to bring metaphors to the mongrel bastard tongue—

There are walls in the mind's time, and
I would live in the breach.
I would crack myself open to what?
       (Coolidge)

—and make a few notes to put out there, and practice the virtue of interference like two beams of light that make unlikely patterns on a screen, bands of light and dark, black and white, when they traverse a slit, a rupture in a plate that blocks other particles and yet does not purify, because each band speaks to "the nowhere that is also now-here" (Palmer) and beside the discursive point, just oblique enough to suggest the common ground between self and other and to say it is otherwise, an ongoing fluctuation of transit, the press of migration, the whisper of violence in the fact of Cambodians, Salvadorians living in Northern Virginia and Rhode Island and Washington, DC, America as an archipelago of ethnicities strung from North to South and transverse over the flat of the continent, America as a scampering from wars that scatter, make diasporas, ongoing diasporas.

More Than Once in Caves

Once, fast along the ridge, we stopped where bush opened
The bones in a pit eager to enter the fuselage of our talk
The swerving of terrain, awake to the measure, the iron of its eye
I tried to pick out the moment when calm went south
And you the girl beside the ridge, a huge breadfruit tree
With balls of fruit, like soccer balls, the pimples are also green
I came from the tree and stood beside you like a vine
To crawl upon the main trunk where the sun sat like Jesus

Once, in deep anguish, the ridge buckled and left us
Steel pipes ran beside the cave where we made fishhooks
Of bone, the debris living with us, a rock with blood on it
The tableau with ankh to protect our backs from the heat
O thief! I went home from the ridge, a mountain lion
Circling the wood pit, the cave was of bone, the fire not yet come
To dynamite the hill as we angled towards its mouth
I waded among the splinters of a water fight, out onto Crete

Once, in archipelago, a necklace tied with water, a fuse lit
Brought us into the cave, it shut like a footlocker on our plight
Forced to huddle, we waited for a fire, we sucked gas
And dreamt of smoke and drew pictures of copulation, I went
Beside salt marsh in Guinea, or under stars, of the roof hole
You brought in dyes and set paintings on our left
The rooms lie still, the noise of your breathing in my head
Man in a cave beside a fish bone hook, woman beside a cave

Once, we saw that it was night, the cave opened out of a hill
The rains came, and phonemes sprang new from the ridge
People left for grasses east of the Nile, and I was left
A shell of crab on my back, a crop of wool for my head, gear
Of lights deep over the grass, we ate from each other's hand
Choice meats were stored beside the pit of wood for your trek back
And I took to my bed in thorn, and rain wet me from the roof hole,
Next day we planted out a canefield, I begged you to hand me up

Once, when begging was invented, we sat out the fire and winded
I touched your palm-print to my palm for the need of a self
The cave beside a mound of slag, we made hooks of iron from this kiln
The salt mines of Liverpool, the coal pits of Dahomey, the benches

Of courts with smooth bars for the plea, you on the steps
I went up to you when begging was the norm, when the cave was burnt
Poking through the ash, you to the camp of refugees, I to the holding pen
The men went out to plant with their hands what grew in that place

Once, I returned from your neck where my face was on fire
To dig up the roots that grew under earth at the earthworm's back
I picked apples with the daughters of sons, I bought a transistor radio
To you I gave every penny of my sweat till the plantings were done
I looked at sun, straight at it for once, to see if I could stand god's mouth
Went east with the cargo of my doubt, the cave was flooded
We turned back then, to snow beside the hooks made out of our colloquies
There were five of us: two of us were mules, three men in a cave

How easy to be alone when the wind insists, the bones we collect
As easy as digging up the hole, the spirals of talk you make out of wind

Aphrodite of Economy

Landscape, as the events of a prior discontinuity,
will never know what we make of it, although
telegrams come, and breath hurries, at the top of a rise
to survey the orderly valleys, the young cane
and the mixed shoots, some as tall as a man,
and miles of them going back into another century
of uniform labor the color of earth.
Anyone can break the code to take out the truth
because it is there, so long as there is an eye.
Language is different. History chokes on a rag of kerosene
the fuse is lit down a corridor of echoing images
and one cannot shuffle the fulgurating words
to nominate as aesthetics what time calls blood—
though once, it was thought, once—and a woman
doubled over and coughing must signal the scar
of cutlasses, diseases of the womb that maim the adult.
What do the fields represent, the harvest?
ratios, roads, drainage—the plucked flower of science—
these words are fuel to tinder, they promise
extremes of hatred if not boredom with the text
we were born to desecrate, and that's the paradox
of being from an offshore rig: how to put out
the wide savagery when you're inside the beast
that in other legends, as wolf, swallows the community
in this one has left prints in the form of sugar cane
that actually broaches a goddess of slave economy.

Some Days in the City

Some days, the sky descends to the level of mid-thigh water
the clock-hands come loose, and language is a skiff
over land through the rhythm of your breathing, girl
then I can hear the pink oriole, the body is a metronome
of blood and syllables beating placentas of speech
and news tingles like a caress of words still to be spoken:

umbrellas, bracelets, sleepers in doorways, police and victim—

I wind these objects to strike my human self dead
so as to taste the massy hive, the bloom and sounds
following my spending to gather up the pennies, kisses
meant for you, lost in transit, I follow my own kisses
to rooms in European cities, to the bottom of a shot glass

like a piece of economy flung about the streets
I spit pronouns, you fall from my lips, bewildered
I fall to the tracks, a suicide, a trembling drunk at
Du Pont and this day is a book left ajar, next to the rain.

Prayer to Shadows on My Wall

Soon the rush-lights will go out in the flesh
of sympathetic bodies once close to my own hand
and I will go to my hammock, thinking of little
except the numbness that alone makes bearable
the wind's twisting. I want atoms to separate
like hairs or dust onto the heads of my daughters.
I want to violate the edict that traps my hunger
in cages and away from her rough shoulder
and once to be enough for this and all the loves
that flicker through my bedroom before sleep.
They keep me awake, and tonight they are fierce
as whips or as needles to make the skin crawl.
I want to drift like the poui in a southerly wind
and settle where I need to before the faces erode,
my appetite of iron caulking the egg-shell heart.

Time Once Again

Let there be time like the turn of a golden orrery.
—Al Cook

Let there be time for the fields to redeem
the caulked keels and cracked ankles
of slaves dead in seven years of turning
and let the houses topple as the body topples
time's spinning like the turn of a golden orrery

Let there be poetry like an alphabet cut from iron
manacling the pen to paper and to my flesh
to print marks like gashes in time's sleeve
empty in hot sunlight, with the bodies turning
into earth, and earth into fury, in time's comedy.

Au Café Noir

The piano's bone-white oars are pressed
to music of falling water. Her passions
clink softly in the courtyard, and a Venus
entering the bath, rocks gently on his notes.
The waves fall from her rough shoulders.

A blush of body rises on sleeping trees.
Caught in the tide, they sway to the brink
walk over leafy rivers to the white basin.
Their own foot soles are the rocks: a bridge
of notes like earrings on a tinted stream.

Coracle bears the acolyte and his mistress
in tremor of arms, off from the recital.
Camisoles, a residue of decomposing bars,
bloom in the center: *Mater saeva Cupidinum*,
hidden among the rocks of Leonardo's genius.

Toward morning, the brush is put in water.
A peep from the radiator: then choirs rise
flutter in the yard and stevedores begin
unpacking heads, sweeping away the litter.
The iron chairs arrange themselves at table

and nymphs come down from the pediment.
Summer over the yard went with the tide.
Flutes are put up, the piano is a ship
but no paddle or slaves to work the bones.
I drink café noir to buck up the sunrise.

jenny mueller

artist's statement

My writing is changing. More and more, language is a source of solace for me, as a site simultaneously of absolute freedom and of adherence. I used to write out of a love of people and also out of a sense of enthrallment in some physical environment (urban or western). But lately, more and more, I feel I write as if I could say something *to* words, through words, and that perhaps I have been doing so all along. It is a matter of survival, somehow, since in speaking to words you are addressing the thing that makes you human. When we are in writing, we are like dogs that twitch in sleep as if they are running— in the dream of being what we are.

The dream includes extinction, dementia, silence, the reach for a language of the outside. I have written more about these things than through them; I have put persons and places in their stead as a means of writing to them— though also perhaps because I loved the persons/places. Love, that old motive, is probably what drives me back to "lyric" forms of address (although I have never really understood genre classifications anyway). At the same time. I would like to write a poetry that is truer to the polysemic disfiguring actions of language. My means of doing so has been through that charismatic failure, the lyric "image": invisible and warping between image, icon, and symbol, an and/or/not rhetoric that pushes toward the furthest silences in words.

But that last bit already sounds false, and I had not intended to sound so much like an Archibald MacLeish poem. The more I write, lovingly, to words, the less interest I have in "finishing" or "originating" individual works. Writing is reading, not mastery.

Fisher Towers

To dream about tremors is a salt dream
The dream of the palo verde, rushing its allover green to a singeing light

is salt passion for palsy, the father's
confusion at the arid towers, senses all walking
in different directions, the last day memory serves as your wife

The dream of the mind: dementia, the father
come a calamitous length on the body's sea

eye ear touch each develops an angel of furious doubling sword: the mirror
forgets your dummy, slaving for Zion within its mines

Just as in dreams he is always completely
false and intact, fresh-dipped, new-
skinned in the spalike cures of the dream,

speaking as it seems without images—father,
there is no cure. Shaking does its flylike to her hands, his speech
sprouts bright flat feathers as it fails, newsmen explain how this last

was a sugaring of Carthage. That is not sugar
I taste on my lips but a ghost that forestalls
to descend, that threatens to make me its tongue.

Betrayed by KC

The whites of the city spill out. Go.
I like how the snow

burns like both the blister
and the fever-forced body;

I hate how they plow both away.
I wish it could be

my righteous, bitten brother—
a nickname only the two of us know

stops us from making
any other sense. Go,

Tonio, Gustav
Aschenbach, loving the little blonde boy.

My brother the snow stuttered
s/s/s/sister. Said this time

we're both going to fall.
Then tunneled my head

with 20,000 days of excaved scrawl,
an ice-age graffiti. What's left

is illegible
carbon copy. And something

invaginated, something
with sound.

Bonneville

Well I skated toward a star
on Lake Bonneville.
Till silver and cursive boiled off, and I stood
shimmering in a salt garden.

One by one
all love's figures are whited, but a picture stands outside
of the blinds, like the stubbornest
O. Look how the rock bases
crimp off the scorching floor, in a lift-off
of bodies. So
one divines in an arroyo.

What is more or less like

than sloughing off likeness.
Millennia shuffling blackjack hands.
Disclosure so straight
it shows the world's curl,
how cool vision drains to firing dial.

But still I imagined an animal's flight
up past the literal harvest of salt
on the day they brought his blood coat to me.

Diorama

Take a rib of light

and let it be the handle for the wreck,
turn it in the bed of masonry.

Someone cast a row of bikers,
set them down like molded soldiers (pink

and black with heat) in front of Main
Street Memories and the 1912 Emporium.

I can see them out the window of the Tokyo Hotel,
across your drawn, smoking cheek.

In the long light, you're
italic. We are sealed
in a specimen jar. The moon is afloat

in the summery sky, like the worm
inside the bottom of the gold
mescal. This

little history. This
little model

town hall. I don't need to tell you
what evidence we are.

Here now my hands
make a ledge of your back, fingerprints cooling

inside the cracked stone, light
casing over, a hardening age—

The story tells how one girl's finger bone

set seven brothers free.
My brother, I won't mourn your death in fire.
Under the ashes, a skeleton key.

Life in the Comics

Something is laying its hand on this hour.
Gridding the sky now and stepping the lake,
holding off nights flood erased the lake drive—
everything's live
transmission. How does your speech
arise? In bubbles, like water and blood,
but hanging in its white gallery of light
with the atomite soul of detail. Speak to me,
over the frames. The good are estranged into rules;
the bad are stuck licking their lips
on an old avenue—always angling downtown,
crossing the heart at the same intersections—
and fall off the face of the story
whenever they made a blind-
alley turn.
           Mother can I go
through the rip in the weather now, please?
The mouth that's so wet in spring.
By the river they went picnicking, young Socialist Realists,
till somebody turned toward the city to scream.

Peninsula

Delirium was: to fall from the furrow
and seek as we did the chill
white shore. The water
played in a tape loop. Behind, the park hissed
like the park in *Blow-Up*, a tape
hiss—the pines started ringing
like glass. We'll want
to return here: we'll want
to play back. In the chilly hotel,
to have *breakfast in fur*.

Darling the campgrounds
are sodden abandoned, their sites
bitten in and the paths
steeped in cold,
chemical soak.
An etching, a darkroom
developing. We come in and flick on
a switch, find ourselves
in a circle of technicolor mosses. This
then will be our moss bed.
The rain doesn't touch us; we have on
film skins. And come out
restored: coldslicked & florid
of eye.

Upper
peninsular. Lastly the state
scrolled past its own names & flowers, finally
flipping at the water's empty reel.
I want not to rest
again anymore, in this speech
only half-soaked in pictures.
Midnight excursions on the liquid paths
to the cordoned
ribbon falls, hikes to the park's
high balconies (the chasm
points always deemed *scenic*, love)
where rapturescope lights
came off your face,
through which panorama spread in fire.

Portrait of My Father as the Boy of Winander

The visored may
apples, tenting their sexes and bells in low camps
at the bottoms
of wood, did they demand

more stopping, more
piety; must the visible
world be remade as a purity lifted
for flag, a blood

that is waved before children?
After
all they hid, they
marched and were zoned

like any organism, prone
to swallowing acts. Shouldn't we have simply
stoned the newcomers,
cut off their naming
tongues and building hands, though I
have these too.

      The may apples went under
pulling their thread from the weave.
They became an unreadable
signature, then
the mirage of that signature.
They went beneath
my tongue.

Come back it is all the same /
Come back it will all be just
the same—so the mother said
to her graved child. My father puts his hand
to the wall, in the house
he has lived in all my life,
where suddenly he looks
for a hidden door.

Still did his mind
have to fall into this watery

mimicry, where he can't
picture himself?
Now he hunts after
the track of slime,
or is it a silver philtre.

Year

Squirrel chase in the bare trees
                                    ribbons

All night the snow spray
twists and collapses
along the house walls and the icicle

spinning its gothic, monomaniacal
tale-that-will-end-in-water

water the creditor trails us
water the landlord builds fences tends and keeps
water the nurse
changes and watches the doctors, the patients

Laura Mullen

Artist's Statement

Where it's at (I got two turntables and a microphone)

1. "Since the First World War Americans have been leading a double life, and our history has moved on two rivers, one visible, the other underground: there has been the history of politics which is concrete, factual, practical and unbelievably dull if not for the consequences of the actions of some of these men [*sic*]; and there is the subterranean river of untapped, ferocious, lonely and romantic desires, that concentration of ecstasy and violence which is the dream life of the nation."

Norman Mailer, "Superman Comes to the Supermarket"
(*Artists, Critics, Context*: 140)

2. "It is a silly thing, to ask someone how you might go about finding out who you are. Presumably you already know. But, in my case, I am of two minds and at least two bodies. Only one is visible to me. The other one I inhabit but cannot catch sight of.

"My dilemma is familiar. I can't recognize my reflection, as I can only nod to the shadows the director has painted on the wall behind me. These painted blobs move in tandem to my hesitations. We could begin to dance, but that would only prove a distraction to those whose attention I have gathered like wool on a spring day."

John Yau, "Boris Karloff in *The Mummy Meets Dr. Fu Manchu*"
(*Borrowed Love Poems*: 46)

"Man's face is a flag"
In *Means Without End: Notes on Politics*, the critic and philosopher Giorgio Agamben clarifies the extraordinarily high stakes which pertain to the problem of being recognizable and recognized. Pressing on the question of representation, Agamben looks into the deadly aporia which opens when—our

ability to see humanity or people (without a definite or indefinite article) blunted or absent—the other falls into a dangerous area of unrecognizability: "When their rights are no longer the rights of the citizen, that is when human beings are truly sacred, in the sense that this term used to have in the Roman law of the archaic period: doomed to death."

Noting that "what is new in our time is that growing sections of humankind are no longer representable inside the nation-state," Agamben finds in the refugee "a limit-concept that at once brings a radical crisis to the principles of the nation-state and clears the way for a renewal of categories . . ." (20–22). I am borrowing Agamben's idea here as hopeful: whether or not the renewal comes 'in time' is unclear. But it is not the figure of the nomad (whose model of willed and seasonal movement powerfully blends nostalgia and exoticism) but the figure of Agamben's refugee that guides me as I attempt to understand the complexities of poetry's restless and ever changing situation. For poetry is sacred. Outside of the apparent safety of silence, as well as the communal garden of "common sense," unable to tell it any other way than slant, poetry is, as Carol Snow says of grief, "to wander." "My indirection finds direction out," I used to quote Theodore Roethke quoting Hamlet, and now I'd add, only to abandon it. Or to be abandoned by . . . ? The poems collected here trace ways I tried or ways that tried me. What I think now is that real poetry is always en route—located in a vulnerable present tense, which implies that there is no belonging on either side of a or the line drawn in whatever medium. Peculiarly situated in transition or as translation, in the "in between," in border zones between possible communities and texts, between the real and the imaginary, partaking of both politics and desire, engaged with life and death, contemporary poetry puts at risk those understandings of identity that Modernism—despite or because of its emphasis on fragmentation—managed to "shore against ruin." High Modernism, we might say, especially the American brand, loses the self only to find it (recovered precisely by and in the threat of loss). It's unsurprising, then, that the work of Ezra Pound, say, as much as T. S. Eliot, lends itself to the uses of an academy that still means (granting or rather selling us our conditional, impermanent, and unequal rights) to make good citizens of—some of—us. What is surprising is that poetry and pedagogy aren't constantly putting each other in question, for the "event" of the poetic, notes Derrida, "always interrupts or derails absolute knowledge . . . This 'demon of the heart' never gathers itself together, rather it loses itself and gets off track . . . it exposes itself to chance, it would rather let itself be torn to pieces by what bears down upon it. . . . No poem without accident, no poem that does not open itself like a wound, but no poem that is not also just as wounding."

What Derrida calls the demon of the heart I relate to what Adorno identifies as a "blind spot." It is in the blind spot made visible by art that we, seeing the failures, the limitations of our vision, see best. "The new," writes Adorno, "is a nonjudging judgment." The blind spot, like the refugee, like the poem, marks a space of vulnerability, where our knowledge can be seen for what it is: "flowing," as Elizabeth Bishop writes, "and flown." No poem, we might say, that does not make of its readers those who—also *wounded,* multiple, restless, and unhoused—open the way for a renewal and revision of categories.

Derrida—in *Che cos e la poesia* (What thing is poetry)—describes the poem itself as a sort of hedgehog, out in the middle of what he refers to as the "auto route" (for Derrida as for Celan the poem is always en route), "rolled up in a ball, prickly with spines, vulnerable and dangerous, calculating and ill-adapted. . . ."

Proust—in *The Guermantes Way*—describes this process: "To succeed . . . in gaining recognition, the original painter or the original writer proceeds on the lines of the oculist. The course of treatment they give us by their painting or prose is not always pleasant. When it is at an end the practitioner says to us: 'Now look!' And, lo and behold, the world around us (which was not created once and for all, but is created afresh as often as an original artist is born) appears to us entirely different from the old world, but perfectly clear . . . Such is the new and perishable universe which has just been created. It will last until the next geological catastrophe is precipitated by a new painter or writer of original talent."

Alba

Dawn where the, where the.
Gray lifting off,
Fog rising, herons on the black mud,
Exposed, of the bay. Blue-grays and greens,
The steady shore, the knife blade
Leaves of the eucalyptus dripping in fog,
Tic, tic, the air salt. Dawn,
Dawn, dawn; the idiot's
Stutter. Remarried.
The mirror slips out. Out
On the glazed mud
The vase-shaped birds make their harsh
Unvarying cries. I am.
Chalk smell, damp, of clay and the dull gray
Swelling under his hands, turning, opens
To a vase. Dawn. The shelves full,
The bisqued and the still-damp squat, O-
Mouthed, all wonder, veiled to be trimmed.
Smell of clay, Dawn, dawn, favored a deep blue
Glaze called cobalt, fired all night
At cone six, or cone ten.
I don't know the trade. The hell
Of the kiln intact, in the dark, a brick
Removed: a window into hell. Remarried.
Up all night for beauty you could use.
I am going to explain.
Dawn the deep blue
Burns away, the fog crawls
Off the edges, exposing
The flesh color, the raw
Clay. The cries of the blue
Gray herons float back cross the bay.
Smell of clay. Dawn. Silence.
Begin again.

Sandbox. 1952.—*Homage to Joseph Cornell*

1.

This is as much of the ocean as we ever wanted.
Framed.
White foam sliding away from a single starfish,
Some ball bearings, and a few broken springs.
We know how to let go gracefully,
The wooden frame a little worn at the edges,
The pane of glass painted with blue lines. . .
These are formalities we were brought up to appreciate.
Doesn't the window own the view?
That's how I love you.
Blindly.

2.

This is a package we don't have to open,
Summer shipped after us, into fall.
"We found some things you forgot here."
(The blue string knotted by spiders or sailors.)
"I bet you thought you'd lost these."
The yellow sand spilled like a scarf
Under a dry starfish and two ball bearings,
Arranged by an astronomy of broken springs.
And that translucent smear of amber along one edge,
A single silk stocking
(Why bother to send it at all?)
Sheer as your shadow, smelling of must and salt.

3.

This is a music box. The ocean breaks
Here in other ways than we know,
Casting its clockworks onto a dry shore
Of cracked white paint and sand.
It has no sound of its own. Like a shell.
You remember the life you left there.
Under glass nothing is accidental;
In mirrors and water it happens twice.

A Series of Failures So That I'm Sick of the Word

Love. *Fucked in the ass*, Proust's heroine says, so he knows what she thinks of him, *you might as well let me get myself* . . . Anyway, sick of the whole thing, even if true, or just because it's true, but repeated, hence cheap, so you feel that disgust you get in a warehouse full of imported stuff. Someone got it *for a song* in some country we're fucking up the ass and it reeks of strange musks, odd, heavy, and then something light and too dry sifted over the baskets—I get a headache fast—small bells, the click of beads. Ritual carvings for nothing, somebody saying, Wow, look at this, but not buying. Sick of myself, probably. Not taking anything home, not keeping anything. I nearly killed myself over a man I can't even be bothered to write a letter to now, stumble across in a drawer the foreign coin he gave me I wore the color off into my skin all that summer. Bins full of frogs that dance or play weird instruments, broken altars with nobody home, stacks of delicate rice-patterned bowls, empty and cupping each other. Everything here proves a life I can't share, imagines the body I'm stuck in. Adorn it, adore, and a door, maybe another way in? Eating off "China," looping Italy's gold around my neck, sleeping under Mexico, brushing my legs the brilliant flicker of India-dyed gauze, taking Cambodia home to hide the palm's cheap plastic planter. I don't take anything home. Don't you get sick of the good find forgotten with each new one? So that you suddenly see them again, in some drawer or corner and without that thrill you can see this was the wrong country, that they had been used to celebrate something you won't ever understand. Even the men I stay friends with make me sad, love, the word itself is an ingeniously carved stand of dark teak portraying the whole garden, the circle of ornate figures all facing the wrong way, seat for some spider-armed alabaster god, or something. Somebody made this thing, somewhere, and I want to see the hand that held the knife, or pushed the shuttle through the web to make this pattern, there where it's weaving in the heat, the long bus ride, where it means the strangely close mountains, the curious shade of greenish-blue at the top of the sky, a language I can't make the smallest sense of at all. So that I'm lost in something larger than myself and not for once fucking anyone over but utterly lost and losing myself far enough.

The Catch

Sat in a faded teal-blue chair above the sea to watch.
The sea the same color, but a line of more vivid azure
Farther out. There was a fisherman, hands in the pockets
Of his loose pants, lounging near the pole he'd planted,
Thin tree, in the stones near the edge of the white
Surf it bent towards, suddenly. He pulled out a small fish,
Gray, silvery; worked it free of the hook and dashed it
Down hard on the gray beach; then he flung the invisible
(Except as a quick glint, and gone, of light) line back out.
At his feet the light flashed up twice and then lay still.
There were blue shadows in the white where the waves
Broke, and where they were hauled back out the wet rocks
Shone. Further down in the dazzle a swimmer lifted
A glistening arm and then rose, dripping: brought back
His jeweled body to dry land and the dull, but slowly—
The weight, the awkwardness, returning. At the foot of the sea-wall
He stooped for a towel, scrubbed at his body roughly as one
Watching himself watched touching himself touches himself:
As though it were not his body, quickly; the despised
Shoulders, thighs, buttocks . . .—brought back. Almost
Transparent, "ghost-like," *like an after image*, the edge
Of the Alps in snow, above the town, hovered . . . floated . . .
The edge of the white in the blue, which echoes; *almost
Transparent.* The eye glitters, the line tightens . . . .

Stopping By

How to stay here in evening the snow
Enclosed space I am myself
This side outside of silent another
Promise muted darkening

Woods words worlds
Shimmer this dissolve of icy
Flakes whirling down
Where I stopped to speak around me

A version encountered on the edge
Of a property I recognized
As the belonging of another
Vanishing or slowly being erased *death*

One of the interpretations, certainly. . .
What I opened my mouth on
Might have been the cold burning and bitter
Stuff flung away by a turning lathe

(Another moment the machinery
Of night made) I got in the car
And drove away
I got back in the car and drove away

Frames

1. *Refusing to Face*

Empty or "empty" under title: part
Of street; edge of lawn; side of house
Hand drawing   Thought balloon: boiling overhead
A door open / shut   I didn't admit [at least]

Sign advertising distance

                               Hand clasped to mouth for regret

Interior: window: frame
Parted speech
Mourning: stilled: incomplete Hovered over the head:
                               Hindenburg-like

Door ajar, negative and positive   Exterior: *"For a long time I*
'Beside myself'
In one a widening (or narrowing)   Large eye close-up and tear
Line of darkness / light   X'd out tear

Into bits

Frame full of fragments   Window: snow (widow)
                               Interior: obscuring view
Lines on face meaning   Of "empty" street [part]

Who will lead us home caressing
Left to right   BOOM: fire
                               In jagged *linga sharira*
                               Ground anxious
                               Figure

Sign: Elect
Word obscure
Next   Frame:
                    "A vote against uncertainty!"

Side of house angle of sky what might
Next

                               Bubbled away above the heads of the
                                    gaping
                               Crowd the blank 'thinking' as of used

Oxygen: bloop bloop bloop

Areas of erased
'Rescued from the image' as if

"Meanwhile"   Caw-meantary, wing-shadowed

Exterior: white out
Interior: widowed speech   "The End"

Close up: the edge of the lifted
Halo of exclamation
Points

2. *Recount*

Held up to the light light inscaped little new moon fingernail paring of if I
changed can I burn my mind and read close edge where cuts slip onto
floor under table tally when you're out out waiting it up as if to grasp but
unsteady stack tilted in frame and pencil at counted twice then subtract
"1 . . . the repose of 2 / . . . the foolishness of numbers" blue pricked into
permanent flesh due process spilled what looked they like meaning just
not quite stepped off mentally dusting but blacken entirely having thought
or join divided borders or punch if to toss to cast in untidy "if you could
see this you wouldn't" tested adherence use value yes no and finger
finished not listen on any list

3. *Tragedy*

Somewhere in the equatorial   Caption: Caution
Locating us

Some tear in
Overhanging leaves   Obscured
                                                          To explain or suggest

Wilderness   ['happy savages']

Arrows   Interior: hand on telephone
                                                          Answering / hanging up

Interior: done orientalist
On walls and floor the heads
And hides   Thought balloon:
           "Exploratin' the American myth!"
Extinct   Silencing sequentially
                                                          'Floated' testimonials

ART   [thou?]

From the products
Of the taxidermists'
BOOM: feathers 'snow'
Through frame

Interior (close-up bird's eye vu):
Telephone
Claw-like hand
Extended
Sleeve of suit jacket frayed cuff
Swastika cuff link
Number tattooed on exposed wrist

White raised scarification
Evidence
Of suicide attempts
The hatching
Of a text: *Held up to the light*

Drumming fingers for impatience
Caution: "Will the Dead Speak?"

Interior: as in [the] dark, d'arc

Set flag of overheard speech
Settled fate

Next: the air-port
Next: a cleared space ['in the forest']

Close-up: eyes
Reflected fire

He covers his mouth as if to cough
To catch what might
To read the results [final] into a tiny
Receiving device

Central frame: turning reels

Wavering into the air recorded singing
As cloth shaken out above a reach

O-sagekenu seebythe dawnsurly

Profile lips to [kiss]
The depending
Teat of that hovering blank

4. *Crux*

Interior: white line of draped recumbent
Figure; vertical shadow

Separates

Arriving / departing

Close-up: oratory: air-port
    "A negative space distorted to reveal
      The contours of the
Filled in as in fully inked
Widow of the frantic to complete   One word

Shiver   Lines around the bodies for
Frame: the torn
Fragments "an unknown number"   End frame:
Shiver: is it cold in this frozen space   *Next week: 'Wake'*
Or is there something you'd like to confess?

Applications of

A surface removed. Or an "I" here, as in *I*

Applied the (red)
Paint and then   scraped it off.

As in with my (bare)
Hands . . . .   Or applying again for

Painted (a vermilion), let it
Dry in part (the color dulling) and then *partially*

"We cannot encounter the actual face"
The belief in the actual face
Through   On the other
(Returning)   side of

Shut the door she'd fleeing (locked) on the other side of
Which (invisible) she called out his name she called out

"[A]s in *I*"

In the areas defined by the off-center vertical black line residual signs of a
frantic insistence and then—in time where (roughed in) this—an equally
frantic regret. History of. Who wrote.

To be thought of as self-
Correction. To get *closer.*

I or to the read. Applied myself.
Or applied to the red *Apple Red.*
Read. As (if) it applied. My.

Application (another one).

A description of how the money would.
And if with the other end of the
Brush, as if inscribing there a secret
Text, too dense to read, abraded

In lines between lines

Or the sound of the resistance, it had dried some by then it wanted to stay
by the time I had changed my mind as we say, urgent, whispery little noise
it made I was leaning close breathing the dust I made like a request for
money a hopeless desperate request a psst, pssst, cht, cht, cht, or like the

character, in the story taken slowly in front of us structurally apart "for meaning," revealing the "secret shame" on which the whole plot, discovered now, down to the bare worn or what hunger behind the wainscoting and I stepped back imaginary hat in my imaginary hands so to speak and frowning in this light hurry changing grave pressing import signify tell no one telling urgent hissed voiced youarenot youarenot youarenot or theytheytheytheytheythey won't. They won't.

Scraped or clawed it off.
Got it off of there don't.
The track as if dragged.
Sorry as if falling failed to.
As if tried (and failed to).   Stop. (Stop.)

As if subtracted not even able to what exactly

Or they were saying "You might be *more* you on the medication"; We are a collection, he said, of chemicals; I stood from the work frowning back for an instant noticing only then

My hat (as if applied) had a hole in it   held out

In this light. In this. In this.   Stop.

Decay. Dissociate.

To come or go to pieces to be so to speak

Scraped down to the fabric itself and tried to loosen for the tight weave
To make it cough up (so to speak) or disclose

Oh the *meaning* came clear enough
Pocket change or *a little ready*   (Stop.)

I couldn't I kept saying even *feel* anymore. (Down to the emptied accounting the single bar of dust-lively light escapes.) (When I say "I" on what side do you put yourself?) Past the possible to face . . . .

And anyway he did finally get self-conscious or uncomfortable about
    talking about

Disintegrate.

Anyway stained the threads   (Loosened, listen)
Finally (down to) the repeated
Applications of (and past) *This*   (right through the)

Not this.   (Impoverished representative of)

Looking *as if.* With empty hands. With bloody hands or hands bloodied by the attempt. Someone had tried to climb back up or claw single-minded wordless *the* or *a* way out. "Like a rat," she said of how he with her arguing "desperate" at the end was trying to leave: "the relationship." But they *chew*, he said. Cht. Later. To someone else. Rats. "Or an 'I' here . . . ." (As in *"couldn't even . . .":* the part he said cut.)

Leaning specific open into which
The reader both does and does not
Place himself or herself   "the actual"   (broke)

Down the single dense deliberately painted dividing line (locked) on either
Side slightly differing traces (of) versions of what could look like another failed

(Failed) (or I was) application

To (leave a lasting record or)
Close. Close

amy newman

artist's statement

A Preface

Metaphorically, I am comprised of glass: part container, part reflector. As with Stevens's jar, when I place myself in the world, the world rises up in a kind of order, a wild no longer entirely wild for my having observed it. I wonder how much of writing is reflection in a polished surface, and how much of me shows back the world untouched by my imaginings. A love of writing is a love of the world, is true faith in the world, continuously challenged: begrudged, hurt, but continually forgiving. This morning on the long table: a tulip petal fallen from bloom. It is "beautiful": *adj.*, having beauty. Very pleasing to the eye, ear, mind, etc. Soft and flat at its end, curved on the sides as a tongue, colored in running stokes of dark pinks, gossiping to reds. Does nature teach us beauty or do we invest the natural world with our perception of the beautiful?

When painter Roy Lichtenstein defines art as "perception of reality," he speaks of the complicating, intoxicating call for the near-impossible, the magic trick of representation: a desire to capture the moveable world with a tool that might always seem somehow inadequate. Painter Marlene Dumas speaks with loving irony when she says of the limiting canvas: "Why do painters still paint? Because the world is flat." In the physics of writing, one records the order of flux and experience—world plus observer—in language. Reality is not out there, static and waiting: it's in how the perceptive jar feels the world rushing up to it, those vines and trees now calculated in symbols and movements like algebraic fiends, digitizing themselves at an incalculable rate. Language is as dense as paint, as flexible, as vastly hued, as multireferential: words look pretty, calm and prim, and love their little curls and serifs, their italics, etc., but there's a lot of hypertextuality going on between ink and fiber.

The problems with representation also fascinate the painter, and this fascination absorbs me. In Rembrandt's *The Anatomy Lesson of Dr. Tulp*, the doctor compares the open, gasping space in the cadaver's left arm with the reticulation of his own live one. But more than inspection of the *flexor digitorum superficialis* muscle interests the doctors and Rembrandt. They wish to study the body for the source, the spirit, the stimulus, the electricity that animates us from simple flesh and vivid bone to living in the world. They will come to a point where they will encounter absence: such incapacity is built into this particular search. Rembrandt's painting of this autopsy always reminds me of the iconography of Thomas probing Christ's wound: *How can I come to know this? How close can I get to understanding, to believing?*

Manet's *Copy after Rembrandt: The Anatomy Lesson of Dr. Tulp* is a study of the shift to the modern world, an attempt to locate more specifically the artist's real subject. His presentation of doctors and cadaver is less distinct, blurred to mere washes of paint that barely form faces, clothing, hands, the subject of the art having moved now to another near-impossibility: representation in strokes of colors on the flat surface. As important for Manet are the paint and canvas; these too are part of the world. The action is closer to his hands.

The tulip petal comes to me in images and apprehensions for which I must find virtual symbols from a book of symbols lined up in alphabeticals, definitions, little presentations claiming to hold the entire, a relic of the fall. In my dictionary, the word *fall* has seventy-two definitions, which span a narrative drama—from the creation of the world and the subsequent exile of its first inhabitants, through the downward movement of the human body in its surrender to illness and the world's gravitational pull, to the beauty in the descent of spent foliage in autumn. Perhaps in paradise words actually glistened and coiled and flexed. But there was no need for vivid books to hold the little things.

I love the dictionary, as does any writer. Over and over again I forgive its tiny lie of harboring all possible expression between its pages. The dictionary is my hope, a comrade in the imminent, the gerundive, the act of apprehending. The language of a poem attends to living in this world, with all its complications and intensities, and so attends to the very gesture of defining. The downward motion of a petal as it leaves its bloom may stand for all things perished and perishing. Both the landscape it falls through and the language we will use to render it are vividly alive, yet saturated with memory and loss. With their rich inadequacies, with restlessness and ever-reachings, words are containers and reflectors of a search for that which animates us, which makes the blood continue.

The Architecture of the Wings

Everything vanishes. The line of rain
traverses the country. A certainty of rain.

Behind it, the narrative oceans,
at our backs the longing, the cold sweat

of winter. I say *The lake has a vagrant current*
drifting toward the possible

I say *the subsequent sun on its skin is*
the second language of platinum.

Tiers of white quarried by silence or
an alliteration of angels.

Everything about it vanishes.
Sapphire comprehending white

in the vault of wings,
twilight's outstretched torso

down the noon from which
cold blue has fallen,

the safest indulgence into the air.
It is an accident they are

so beautiful, so severe.

Darwin's Unfinished Notes to Emma

Actually Darwin's gradual loss of faith, which he downplayed for fear of upsetting his
devout wife Emma, had . . . complex causes.
—Richard Dawkins, River Out of Eden

The world this morning is wide as this sea,
and full of potential. I think of you so often,
with great sadness at our distance.

*

Some of the plants I see are extraordinary. One,
whose petals seem lined with cream
and opens out so full
reminds me of your hands . . .

*

It is a diverse world, Emma, the structure
is breathtaking. We will never unlearn these
hours of facts. The world . . .

*

I think of you especially as we observe the orchids,
those flowers that you so admire. I would like to give you
all the varieties of orchid

*

Bees cut holes and suck the nectar
at the bases of certain flowers, which,
with a very little more trouble, they can enter

at the mouth

*

The mistletoe depends on birds to spread its seeds, the
flowers depend on insects, it is all
a series of increasingly apparent
relationships. Nature moves
in profitable steps.

To propagate, the orchid,
I am flustered to write,
requires the cooperation
of the male wasp, and so resembles

                    *

~~we have acquired some idea of the lapse of time;~~
~~the mind cannot grasp the full meaning of the term~~
~~of even a million years~~

                    *

Do you remember that one morning I smelled of nectar?
Darling, the world is feral, and we are natives.

                    *

Of all the species of bee,
only the humble-bee can visit the common red clover.
It has to do with curvature, with length
of the proboscis, too slight
to be appreciated by us. Whole fields of red clover

offer in vain their abundant supply
of nectar to any other bee. This idea

of a vast spread of fresh green waiting
with all its juice,

                    *

Instinct! The mental processes of animals!

                    *

To propagate, the orchid
requires the participation of

the male wasp, to get the pollen
on his legs, and to get him to transfer

the pollen to other orchids.
The orchid must resemble genitalia,

a female wasp, her body,
so the insect will copulate

with the flower. The orchids had to become
desirable, so this man wasp

will alight from one to another,
cross-pollinating. She wears her color

like flesh, and scents brazenly
for him: spreading herself in the cooler air;

her sweet interior; the fumbling
of the dizzy wasp. This did not happen

as a whim. This is
an extremely intricate subject.

*

The similar framework of bones in the hands of man,
wing of a bat,
fin of the porpoise,
leg of the horse

*

I am remembering your subtle throat, how in the heat
your skin will almost pearl. Underneath your dress of skin
all that fragile blood. You are this morning

a field of clover, and I feel drawn to this,
a humble-bee. I am carried in the world's
mouth

*

The same pattern in the wing and the leg of a bat,
in the petals, stamens, and pistils of flowers

*

This is a matter of perfection, over time,
and complication. Did the orchid have the means
to think itself into seducing, to adapt as idea
the perfect dress of reproduction,
the female wasp

a bit of fur and soft petal
curved like its soft parts

*

Last night a dream of you and I dusted in pollen

*

I would like to believe

—**fall back.** To give ground; recede; retreat.

In a series of poems I'm unable to write, a bride displays her interior,
asking a spray of flowers and ribbons to stand for her within,
for her foliate insides, her inner pinks, her whites and her coming losses:
a decoration, a display, an engraving—frilled, flush, wavering

—of her usefulness. Cream roses? Pale Lilies? The powder in the flower,
their heady scents and furry stems surround her, chiming. Lily of the Valley:
tiny wedding bells ringing like a corona about the bigger blooms.
And in its whiteness, or, *And in its vivid blush*,

the day begins. As I have thought in my imaginings. She steps
into delicate slippers, she runs to the camera, she declines toward the ground
and its manifestation of grass, toward all of what it means.
I'll give you this: I'm imagining. It was years before I would be born.

The photograph's flat lexicon's ungiving, its betrayal
of dimension. It could have been raining. They had to have loved,
given love, like fresh ideas, and the doorway behind
them swings out, in a ceremony, and all of the people

throw, I don't know . . . rice? Seed? The metaphor: Multiply.
Fruitfulness. In that arithmetic of culture. Surrounded by flowers,
carrying flowers. Enraged were the flowers, at their most heightened—
sexed and prepared to be beautiful, vivid, their symbolic openings.

My mother and father were married, and walked among the guests,
among the arbor, and found their bodies later slipped of clothing,
cool, rung to each other. The many, restless conjugations they would make,
against which, from a distance, perceptively curved,

the earth appears in miniature: lifelike, petalled, tossed, and floral, in midair

—fall for. *Informal.* **1.** To become infatuated with; fall suddenly in love with. **2.** To be tricked or deceived by; be taken in by.

At first not frail because she was younger. At first comprised
of flesh and thought, brim as a basket of nectarines
and the lovely things of girldom, pearled, strong,

against the deciduous seasons, their losings of leaves,
their going away, a chastening, their slow descent,
baptizing the ground on which the solid flesh

walks out, conflicted: satisfied, yearning.
Against the long stem of flawlessness, they married,
and little girls threw petals, whites and reds

fluttering beneath the eye, sailing, cadence
like the inside of a woman, where everything is secret,
where everything returns, her envelope, her awning, the fertile,

furtive clock of her, inner pinks cloistered,
and full of prayer, oh how the body wants to be.
Against the illusion of the grassy world,

how it curves when you drive on it, promising,
untying the unseeable, the unbelievable, as it emerges: who knew?
The earth slopes down. Within the *yes* of her she is a lake,

ruddle of animal, holographic, the *yes* of her dwindling
under her canopy of skin. Inspired, the husband answers,
dressed only in his coat of wants, his teenage *yes,*

the customary planet of the body's hard attention, his love for her.
And parting her legs out of homesickness, the blind eclipse
of them, against the sky's departure. The many interpretations,

ciphering. *Not noticing, because not looking*? or
Not noticing, because not there yet: the inviolate,
indelible tattoo of cancer. It undulates,

displays itself in fracture, its geometric love of digging in
like a bad luck, a tracing of the Fall. The tragic earth
slopes down, and I express a wish in air:

the sufferings of loved ones iridesce,
turn out to be transcendent, traverse the earth
like an embroidery, illuminate, emblossomed.

And reckless, invisible, I await the bloom,
her body among so many. But I see her:
pale, extraordinary, glorious, simplified: entire,

unadorned: lost of that birthmark:
relieved of that stain: and something of a dream,
something of a written dream.

—fall under. To succumb to; come under an influence or power.

Outside in floral, vegetating thought,
the empty spaces fill with world.
The fitful budding of the columbine,
and intricate, demure, wild growth that wanders
where it wants. Day lilies sugar up in blur.

These scarlets and these yellows tongue and hover
in my version of the world. I try to notice lilies,
try to paraphrase their blooming.
(*The blossoms lift like children;*
they look up.) I tell them

how the words I use are useless,
and the dragonflies form laterals in air:
their spider's web of body, touching down;
and still they float around in parity: their gravity,
the weight of sky. I love their wings

like heaven, glassy patterns in the air,
above the air. Against the upward thrust of earth,
I lay my fragile figure down, eye-level
to the latitude of leaf. Imagine plants,
who promise to remain as if a gift, unwrapped,

but at the season's end they take it back,
and wither, and hardly say goodbye.
Then we are waiting only for the vaster shapes to come,
the bright, descending creatures
and their emblems: their fragile,

lacy wings. My mother was blade-thin,
as thin as blade, and scattered to the wind
as seed, and left us all she had:
the final shell of her, the lace of her,
veined like a wing.

I cannot find her on the earth,
against the breeze, unnoticed, wild,
or the netting of the trees at nightfall.
(*The blossoms lift out of the ground,*
and we look up.) The garden is the dream of loss,

a drift of cell and stem, and gone, a petalled dress
of scent and pollen. Is she among
the far-off leaves and secret trees,
and missing fields towards which I turn,
out of my homesickness as blue as bruise?

Or out of love: that reckless, gentle thing
that hangs its head, that shifts the family leeward.
It torques and fissions, that, which spun me,
slim hot thread of cell division.
(*The sadness of the petals, looking.*)

Geoffrey Nutter

Artist's Statement

A Conversation between Austin Wallson and Geoffrey Nutter

(Austin Wallson is an American poet living in Santo Domingo, the capital of the Dominican Republic. His works include the poetry collection Where Are You?*)*

AUSTIN WALLSON: In the past, you've pointed up what you called the "ceremonial" aspect of poetry. Does that mean you think a poem is like a wedding or a mass, or a ceremony in general?

GEOFFREY NUTTER: A poem isn't like anything.

AW: Remember that time I saw you in Santo Domingo? You looked so frightened. You looked as if your poems themselves were coming up in a foreign place to tap you on the shoulder and say, "Here we are! You can barely claim us as yours; from the moment we are on the page you renounce us. We feel barely any connection to you at all . . . in fact it's almost as if you were not even a person at all."

GN: It's funny you should put it that way, putting the words "You're almost not even a person at all" into the "mouth" of a poem, when obviously I *am* a person and the poem is the nonhuman thing.

AW: Interesting that you should insist so strongly that you *are* a person. What exactly do you think a poem is, anyway?

GN: There is no other way to say it: a poem is, or should be, poetry.

AW: You know that time that you noticed me walking toward you on the street and you pretended not to see me, and you slipped into a church? I followed you in there where you were pretending to pray.

GN: How can you tell whether someone is really praying or only pretending to pray, since both look the same?

AW: I can tell because I was there, and when I am present I know that whatever you are doing is a performance.

GN: But is a performance the same thing as a lie? Is it a pretense?

AW: What do you have to say about your poems that appear in this anthology? Readers are going to want to know a little about them.

GN: A poet is a person who allows himself to be outsmarted by language. A good poet lets the language take him where he never thought he wanted to go. A poet puts himself in the environment of language and wants to be changed by it. To a poet, the color red will only really be red in a poem. And the red in a poem will be the reddest red the reader has ever seen. The images in a poem should strike like lightning. A poem should be the least abstract thing in the world.

AW: Yes, but what does your own poetry have to do with any of this?

GN: What do anyone's poems have to do with what they say about poetry?

The Definition of Swan

One that resembles or emulates a swan
may be rightly called a "Swan," or more precisely
"one who emulates a swan." We may say that he is swan-like.
If he is long-necked and beautiful, or if he flies strongly
when once started, or sleeps in mim,
we may put him to sleep in a swannery.
To "swan" is to wander aimlessly.
Clouds become claws and cover the sun.
An emu on the riverbank is lucent, supervenes.
She eyes the octagons unfolding in the rushes
and finds, when they've unfolded,
the strange eight known as "Swan."
There now. Do they migrate?
Who knows. They float, detached, like constellations,
or a man who pedals passengers along the banks
in a large model of a swan.
Something happens: a woman executes a dive
with her head back, back arched,
and her arms spread sideways, then brings them together
to form a straight line
with her body as she enters the water;
this is called a "swan-dive."
But doesn't it look something like a prayer,
or a way to make love?
It may resemble both, as the clouds resemble crows,
or mountains, or mist in the mountains, or mist minus
mountains, or all of the above.
I wish her name was Cygnus.

Boy Leading a Horse

If you exist; and if, furthermore,
somewhere in the world, this world,
small yellow birds hide in wet leaves,
or other shy, rose-colored, rose-figured
forms; if you once had the power
of being nameless, once, on the day
you were born—then he is looking
straight through you and past these,
and we must, for a moment, agree with
his disdain. You too were once
the tallest thing for miles; you too
were leading or were led through
the imagined and the unimaginable;
you were once this young and fire-new,
you never learned to compromise, like
this earth and sky, and you would never
compromise, like the line that splits
the earth from sky. It is a line
that splits the world in two,
that would sunder your very life
forever. You have felt the sun
and shadows falling on your body.
You have been unspeakably one thing
and unspeakably not and never another;
your world was at war forever.
You too were older and prouder than the sky,
and regarded us this darkly, unblinkingly.
You were something more than human: a boy.
And something powerful walked beside you.
It towers over you still. And it submits
to your control, which you exert with
concentration, with forgetfulness—
with a dark and child-like gesture.

Pastoral

We're passing the whole summer, all of us,
in the country, in a field, where we sleep
under the stars in one another's arms,
with wet grass printing patterns on our hands
where we lean back or fall back into the grass
to sleep under the stars.
                              It's beautiful to be,
and to be outside where the wind is, with the friends
who love you most all summer under stars. And Mary
is there, and another girl too, and so is Milagros Cordero,
and at this moment I'm running toward the others
hand in hand with them, and they're laughing
and Maria turns to kiss me in front
of a circle or a sickle shape of friends
reclining on the earth to show that all is well
and that we are ourselves but not quite ourselves.
We have abandoned ourselves completely
to be completely with each other,
if only for a few moments, to have our only
moment in the sun and be as grass,
green and instantaneous.
                              Why don't I live
this way, where the great yellow disc harrow
lies rusting in the wildly overflowing grass,
and high gazing trees that taper into green points
incline a little in the sky, where they are living
always with the wind, a magnificent thing, and all
that is beloved is evergreen.
                              Listen: there has been
a great storm. Massive clouds have passed before us,
and passed in front of the sun, and darkened
gray-green bridges. We were wading ankle-deep
by sloping green faucets, dark gentlemen were watching
from the windows of a topaz structure,
and air balloons drifted over the heartless craters, tilting
toward Stara Zagora.
                              How were we brought

through the storm like conquerors, made transparent
like petals in the rain, somehow set down gently here?
We awaken under rain-green flags, alive
for a single day.

Pond and Peace

April and Elias. The green month and my brother's son.
Sleep and dream with the lion in his den.
With the lion at your zebra-shoulder, be a zebra, run—
The gentle grass will part for you. Your will has just begun
to be a dark grass that conceals you from the enemies you shun.
You feel them coming fanged on the horizon,
and when they come, come to me, all in the osprey of what you are, or
    what you've been,
or leaving the osprey of what you've done—
As sleep contains a dream, but barely: April and my brother's son.

August is the metal month, an orchid, gleaming alphabet of Z.
What shape do I make so far from you, you so far from me?
It's vague and distorted and why we delay it
is to see how perfect it can gradually come to be.
I try my hand at being a pelican, fishing in the sea
in April, when Elias is an osprey.
Elias and the sea.
Put them side by side like that, and they agree.

And when you have a daughter,
in light green April or zinc-white December,
comets will striate the sky, your father.
And comets will striate the zenith, your mother.
You'll walk down toward the water.
Look! Rain above the river, shriven, silver.
Love you've given over.

The Air War

Some of the things you may be wondering

something like yellow stains on the horizon

as far as you can see, but still they say

wading in the river naked, and we were freezing and hungry?

Please turn to the page indicated

sometimes, but this is only natural, I guess

everything exactly how it was when I left

In mid-air they seem just like swallows

hearing rumors of incidents of torture

We heard that noise from the Red Bridge, and looked

A woman in a brown veil, speaking in tongues

also like rain, so they instruct us to inject

and try to become as children, believing what we are told

looked just as the apple-truck went over. I'll never forget the way

then gradually darker, a blood-orange perhaps

any dissenters, and when one said yes, he supposedly invited him into his
     office,

Ethan? And there were so many apples you couldn't even see the water?

mentions occasional shootings of civilians in the street

then wake up, always as I start to rise into the air, certain I will see her

something to happen soon. We'll see

Right there in the office, with a club or a bat

we trust our equipment to function as usual

faces hidden completely, so we trick ourselves into believing the hands
     reveal so much

photograph peeled from the file, then discarded

always followed by tankers filled with water

they the most delicious apples we ever tasted? So cold from the river

two or three weeks, but probably no more than that

we hear, but so little we actually see

to find out later the driver died on the bridge

The tea is boiling, sky lights up now and then

of her next to the window, eating a nectarine, smiling

fifty-thousand. One hundred-thousand. Two hundred-thousand

and the wet sidewalk, and the flattened leaves. Almost as if November

you think, Ethan, but I hear him sometimes. Wind and sand turn to flocks

    of white birds

and several that have not been explained, so of course we all wonder

constant hum of machinery whose source we can't

and of course pray. The air seems to shout

the thing just over the hill, but sense it's there

but still so beautiful, all those spilled apples

everything hopefully exactly how I left it

Train Station Zoetrope

And wanting to cry his hand beside me,
breath on my shoulder weeds flaring up
through broken screen doors lying in Oregon
fields, places called Jerusalem and "Day Use Only."
And held there, the phantom of him.
This feeling of him, the father, tire tracks in mud,
thriving forest, snow-pastures, colonial
streets. "You are an Arizona . . ."
And how the land
to say to you the way you held there
where a truck disappeared into the water.
Snow baked into salt in the trees, to see
something fall simultaneous with
as it is now. His hand
was announced on my shoulder. I wanted
it always there as evidence that
gingerly through the coils of wire
a lushness was born. The sheep
struck the grass with color. The hand
existed. Stepping along
my shepherd, and when the night was stone,
always having been as complex,
the dam waking up like a cathedral
in the river, to pause and watch
like brave bystanders gazing into the water,
as the truck broke open, and the driver
spilled out. Along the causeway
a forest entitled "Day Use Only,"
could have the sun in his hair forever
at midnight waiting to be permanently
ten miles away from home and further
gently along the platform, slats
of sun coursing breath through the curtains,
feeling him near, as a kind of phantom.
His hand on my shoulder.
Brave bystanders watching.
The truck disappearing.
Sky flicking inside the trees.

Tracy PHILPOT

Artist's Statement

My five-year-old son writes poems, but at his age he calls them "comics" (inspired by the fabulous *Captain Underpants* series by Dave Pilkey). The other night he and I were finishing one of his poems/books: he draws the pictures and then narrates the story for me to write down on each page. While composing, he was observing my cat, Dogar, grooming her curls. Aidan had me write: "Our hero punched the alien monkey with this scratcher" (because Dogar scratched her ear). "Then our hero sat on the couch and licked his underparts." It dawned on me then that this is *exactly* how I write poems, though I don't know if I've ever written a line as delightful as that one about licking one's underparts. Once I was writing about how my husband was driving me nuts and titled the poem "Shackleton In Kindergarten" because I had just seen a film about that Antarctic explorer and was originally using the images from the film in the poem. The poem seemed true to itself, even though it's not factually true. This method may not be particularly sophisticated (since a five year old employs it), but I like being surprised and amused by poems.

Poems for me come from language itself, or images, not ideas. And like my son, I try not to control the narrative process of writing too much. If I write a poem whose language seems flat to me, I may rewrite it from the bottom up, or cut up the stanzas or individual lines to rearrange them. I don't look for a fit necessarily, just a way that the sounds/words/phrases knock up interestingly against each other. I like to move around in the poem until I figure out what it's trying to do.

When I sit down to write a poem I start from my journal, where I collect random overheard phrases, lines I misread from the newspaper, or what I thought (wrongly) a character said in a novel I was reading the previous night before I fell asleep. For years I collected newspaper headlines and magazine advertisements to write with in a modified version of the Surrealists' exquisite corpse game. I eavesdrop on other peoples' conversations, grateful for the gap between my faulty hearing and reality. My poems are much smarter than I am. They know how to have their own life.

I was going to say that writing poetry is something I do to *not* think. But I do think, just not with my own thoughts; I like to use other people's words. I peruse the indexes at the back of biographies I've loved (about Wittgenstein, Diane Arbus, Cheever, Joseph Cornell, etc.). The unexpected is more tantalizing to me, that which I never intended to say or am incapable of saying, than getting a point across or relaying something as it actually happened.

Poetry is my refuge, and because my work as a victim's advocate is so challenging, I often address my own secondary trauma through the act of writing. One cannot listen to other people's accounts of abuse and rape and cruelty delivered by their loved ones without being transformed by it. But recently I tried to change how I write, to make poems that were safer, more objective, more acceptable, to escape the tormented images of the brutality my clients tell me about. I decided I would write about Greek mythology. What I found in reading these myths was more violence against (mostly) women. I do the work that I do because I believe in the social justice of it. And then I write the way I do because I have to. To divorce the images from my brain. To detach myself from their pain. To have language transform haunting stories into things beyond my reach that don't need, that live a different life, that have their own power.

The Rain My Wife

stretched out among the tumult of your voice lie diaries
you wrote for her to have written, blood pink in some south-
ern woman's womb, on the backs of horses, going down over
the Western Ocean the daughter possible was still.

She'll show you this kingdom: the milk sharks flat under
water with food in their mouths, composing despair out
of the children, how small their needs compared to minds.
Grace rides a tall thin neck (mouth) and undersea in the
frontpouch of kelp drinks in the kingdom of milk.

It's easier now to invent: Gauguin beached on horseback,
some people who have moved away for good, imperfectionists—
sleeping with light chests.

In the middle of some celestial adornment of the home,
making the dead look good, relieve a job of meaning, a
reprisal with integrity, say to pay them back for your
disowning them, or even angels sleep in tents.

The rain my wife comes and goes, doesn't ever stay long
enough or past every diamond a spy, every wedding a clasp
on an envelope. Lapping and honed, she's skinless but charm-
ed to reach you, or a year behind you, calling "come in
from the damp porch" while excusing me for thinking you

could be known.
We made some babies on our honeymoon and sold them to get
home. Celebrations in the slave trade.

The hilarity of Resentment Diner, fire-bombing Obsession
Park. It all sounds good to me—thunder of my wife.

The divorced man's dog sleeps on the bed, gets to wear
hose (you nut), and hears your wife fall down whenever
he listens to her. Outside Teton Park, I saw a new moose
walking inchoate, delirious fog.

The wet news, I can never hear it all.

It Was a Boy

As a boat begins its life on the water. Floating,
Would he have inherited a romantic melancholy?
Byronic curls? Or yours, perfect as long fingers?

Lovers are not single people, their intricate
Hands like peach veins, the way the sun makes fruit
Of them. Out of all the musical vectors to nurse,

One was decided upon, but not by us. We can't decide
Between dishes at the banquet, epicureans wanting
A taste of each dish and not having a big enough heart

Or mouth, or having the appetite but not the tongue
To distinguish between the sounds each makes
Of the mouth: the dripping sun, vines crawling

Between the breasts, the precise burgundy of stairs
Roping down into the garden. The boy is behind the house
Without peculiarities, too many varieties of globed fruit.

He waits for the men to return from the fields,
Whatever they work that grows into food,
Rowing toward entire lost families in the lover.

The Clump of Gods

God follows after the days
of the supercontinent Pangea
when the earth had internal disagreements,
broke up, thought better
of its easy wholeness.

Lands rode atop shelves
and took to wandering
across the seas like islands
like incredible boats
carrying more species than Noah
could shake a stick at.

After the land tore god into clumps
they roamed piece discussing with each other
moot points: how many seals
have the gift of gab,
if extraterrestrials have an edge over humans,
who among them is the best lover
granting plentiful orgasms in the night
like forgiveness.

Gods carry trash bags
and gather aluminum cans
saving up for a sabbatical in China.
Their hands are worn
and could not dig through the miracle
of molten earth they created.

While in Africa some build loose nests
in the trees at dusk
next to lowing gorillas.
The gods question each other
before bed to see if they exist.

When the gods dream
they twitch like big cats
and see the supercontinent as Gondwanaland
and wonder if there are other clumps
of gods they must unearth

in Tibet or Micronesia
who'll help them call back
the green or arid earth.

Descriptions (of Living Elsewhere)

like dolphins they narrow toward the end

laughing at the watery edge
of girls, a thin halo of foam
around his lips   what he says
is not holy but momentary, relative to
sound, or sounds of drinking

alone, you know what that sounds like:
    oral kin   exclusion from
  talking

a softening in the hearts
of our enemies, and we have invented things
to abolish essences, ways to tunnel
out of silence into a natural world
that swallows what we leave behind

a late shadow by the rain and I'm afraid
my birth scent is foreign and plain

a bird's voice the size of a needle
okay, I am the clock of affection

On the Eve of Aphrodite

a halo of two eagles chortle
to each other in thermal bands
their wings ensky
an autumn I will marry
my lover
who slaughters a flatfish and cries
in front of his mother
a wild black cat who won't come in
domestic ones lick each other's curls
in a sleeping bag   the sanctity
of tomorrow
will unwad my love
like rosehips titillating a cold month
on the eve of aphrodite
my last card was she who is
a coin of lost children
around my neck
this peaceful season of androgyny
is nature
where only the animal's mate
knows her sexual legs of battle
tomorrow I will ride crisp windows

Thanksgiving

I know the value of water
and gravity, have pushed graves
in a sled up the snowy hill
and eaten entire meals as if
memory

The season of pilgrims and hunting and homes
slides off its lies
constructed to sell it
I guess you didn't remember
how satisfying it could be to keep yourself
alive

When you fly over glaciers that absorb
every calmness but blue
and glide toward the wood stove
you see species crossbreed out of necessity
the reflection in any window could be
yourself

The Constellations of Self

You get comfortable beneath the snow
And then are asked to rise up
To get back into circulation with
Skin worn thin as ancient flannel

I can't make it cling—bunched
Around the knuckles, its slack refusal
To comfort anyone, the emptied woman
In her watching house

I beg you to quit praying to me
Quit haunting my grave, let the squirrels
Haul away the cheap white
Candle of me

For at last my borders are porous: a storm-toppled
Root system, the swallows' circle 'round
Your memory, a backpack of hair,
An echo of your fidgeting inner voice

Calling but I don't know what my name is
Anymore I'm all the homesick birds
Who have ever told the truth
By migrating

A Road Trip as Clues

Poor Cyrene was minding her own mountain
Pursuing her own prey when that prick
Apollo decided (unilaterally) to carry
Her off—Cyrene: not the housewifely type.

The teller of myths dodges the language
Of kidnapping. One minute
You're a naked Lion-goddess the next
Marginalia ravished via chariot.

Talk about reluctant life changes
And going with the flow! Forced into motherhood
She taught her son Aristaeus to hunt
With his giant pupils dilated.

I would tell Cyrene to ignore the ocean
When we walk along its lips
Chattering hard stones that might as well be
A gambler-god's irresponsible die

Each wave losing a new toss
Of diurnal back and forth restless
For some reason it never uncovers
Fluid time it has oceans of.

I would tell Cyrene we all sleep in someone's
Ear. How can she begin gratitude
If he doesn't leave
A space in the hunt?

Cyrene, leavings are more common:
Thrush thrown up into headlights
Of mid-September, mornings gathered
Along dirt roads and bound by internal rings.

She hunts to answer animal language
Entering her empty head. To get free music
In the hills devoid of people.
Her name means fate or bee or plague—

Cyrene, our valley's ripely brimming
With yellow paint poured by no one I can finger.
Fall breathes its death into the cottonwood leaves
Raising higher and higher

The bright flag to winter,
Surrendering us to her shame.
Rattle rattle. Take your chances
With all creatures risked and revenged.

What There Is, Today

Weather's on its way to us.
Dawn is improvising its deep gray clouds
your new round belly makes an appearance

in the kitchen beer's bubbling on its way to us also.
There are packs of horizontal birds
and horizontal loves where once there were

adorations—vertical birds—who showered down
abuse on their faithful students.
In winter there are few birds left.

There are progressions of lies, the way you help me
a bigger plane braving the morning's darkness
followed by a smaller lower plane

whose passengers are more profound because winter.
There's a boat on the bay whose sodium light is pink
and when the water is calm

its reflection is long and untroubled by solstice in Alaska.
My white dog chooses outside
a pile of snow. We have no moths no light for them to be absorbed by—

what draws us is smart talking around music
whose voicelessness thinking day
stays blue in December all day the ships are searching.

What can light or music or even birds tell me on the day
my friend starves, the mother of two lonely children,
who lived a few days beyond her 40th birthday?

The world is too harmonious
to have been knitted by one person too awful
to blame on one.

There is vital coffee sustaining our mornings
and starving its growers. Reptiles are happy
in the flooding down south. Windows a whole skin.

How does the boat know when to turn off its light?
How trust its eyelessness? Shoals, vagrant logs, devoted
gulls and ducks and otters. Saturations of blue winter winter

that same short day my son and I watched the black
dorsal fins of orcas in the harbor. In the absence of anything else
I believe they came for her.

D. A. POWELL

ARTIST'S STATEMENT

The Flesh Failures

Words are the way we call the world into being: "In the beginning was the word, and the word became flesh." The more words we have, the more ways of describing, the more exact, the more power over the world: when a child suckles, he begins to understand that what he wants, that milk, that sustenance, has a name. The first time he utters the name: "baba" for *bottle* (or, if not yet weaned, "mama" for *mother*), he understands the power of language: call for the thing by its name and the thing appears.

Intoxicated by the power of language, the child begins to play with words. He notices similarities between certain words, the way "mama" and "baba" rhyme off one another (though he doesn't yet know the word *rhyme*, he is aware of the condition of rhyming). He creates words for things for which he hasn't yet learned the names. He strings words together into song, gradually developing a syntax by which he might *describe* his experience of being (because he wants someone else to know that he has this power: *language*). And as he continues to grow, he continues to acquire the useful phrases. Perhaps he learns other phrases as well, but they have no practical application, and so he either stores them away or discards them.

Poets continue to suckle at the nipple of the world. They learn more names for more nipples. They hoard the power over all these breasts, feeding at their leisure, at their pleasure. They command an army of mammary, they store them in a box called *memory*, they bring them out like toy soldiers and let them do battle; they are rehearsing and nursing and breaking the rules of war with their words.

This is one way of thinking about why we're drawn to the material of language, as opposed to paint or music or photography or any of a number of other methods by which we might express our passions.

As for me, I know that I felt the power of language early, and I used it as a weapon. I wasn't always able to fight (though lord knows that didn't keep me from brawling) but I could probe someone with language, worrying their armor until I found the weak spot, then jab with a pointed phrase.

So why not become a critic, if all I wanted was to assault? Why write poetry?

Denise Levertov once said of the Language poets that they were taking "a private place on a public beach." True enough, I suppose. But isn't that why so many people are drawn to poetry, regardless of the aesthetic? Because it does have about it a feel of the private. Most poets I know discovered poetry around the same time they discovered masturbation. And probably for the same reason. Poetry gives us a place to explore our passions, to play with possibilities, to open ourselves up to the ecstatic.

And I think this is one of the reasons why we like to speak of poetry in terms of the body. Olson says that "the line comes (I swear it) from the breath." Pinsky says, "The medium of poetry is a human body: the column of air inside the chest, shaped into signifying sounds in the larynx and the mouth." I go back time and again to Longinus, who speaks of sublimity as corresponding to the collocation of the limbs in the body. Or to Whitman, writing that "wherever are men like me, are our lusty, lurking, masculine poems." The poem is the record of the body; how the body experiences the world. Rhythms correspond to breathing and to the systole and diastole of the heart. When Keats writes, "Bright Star! would I were steadfast as thou art," the falling away of "art" mirrors his own expiring breath. And when Whitman writes "sailing, soldiering, thieving, threatening, misers, menials, priests alarming—air breathing, water drinking, on the turf or the sea-beach dancing, cities wrenching, ease scorning, statutes mocking, feebleness chasing," the panting rhythm mirrors the erotic relationship of "We Two Boys Together Clinging." It doesn't have to be spelled out; the quickening breath tells us that this is a passionate embrace.

The body is the first writer of the poem. The mind is that caretaker who moves in to make order. Sometimes what the mind does to the poem is good. Sometimes, it's too much. "I am the enemy of the mind," writes Berryman, while Ginsberg insists that "mind is shapely." With whatever trust or mistrust we have of it, the mind works the poem in a different way. But let's be clear: intellects don't write poems. While they're wonderful to have, they are no substitute for the body's sense of the world. Because the body is *irrational*, and the irrational is where the discovery happens. Keats calls it negative capability. García Lorca says it is the darkness, the *duende*, that it "is drawn to where forms fuse themselves in a longing greater than their visible expressions." Spicer says that we're like radios and the Martians are talking through us. By whatever metaphor we name it, we're listening to the voice beyond the edge of knowing. I say that it is the body, because I know that the body remembers and feels and expresses in a way separate from what the mind does.

Full stops. Broken phrases. Rising and falling rhythms welded within the same line. This is how I shape my poems. Because "silly" meant *blessed* before it meant *foolish*, I let the silly share space with the profound. Hell, I let the silly *be* the profound. We don't know where wisdom will come from; give an open hand to every utterance and let it weigh against every other. All of this voicing arises from the uncertain place that my body inhabits: medicated, rumbling, off-center, uneasy, failing. It's an instrument that needs, with its constant desire to eat, to shit, to breathe, to be cared for—and it is crude and unrefined. But I know by now how to play it, and I do.

[the minotaur at supper:
spare the noritake and the spode]

the minotaur at supper: spare the noritake and the spode
from these ungular hands. goblet stems scattered at my hoofs

a spattering of color on my hide. remnants of one youth
another impaled on my horns: I must say grace over his thighs
for there may be no path back to him. the way is dim and twists

myself am halfboy. am beauty and the end of same: a hungry thing
hunts me also: through which passageway do my nostrils sense blood
what aperture brings me air salted with cries of the ancient corrida

[a mule-drawn scraper packed this earth: levees]

Ode to Billy Joe (1976, Max Baer, Sr dir.)

a mule-drawn scraper packed this earth: levees
mounded into ossuaries. many a first flower
enjoyed the mud and let itself be plucked away
from church picnics. the gathering of men in fields

"what do you remember about the first?"
"I remember the lids of his eyes. the cup of his hand
under my head in the tall grass. a sharp pain
in my guts: I remember saying the words:"

branching from the main body of the river
sumptuous sloughs and overflows: dissipating
potential floods. neither depth nor velocity is attained

under the bridge. half out of the moon. overalls
bunched around our ankles. a shame of a kiss
I cannot stay here: the river opens and swallows me

suppose the clamshell dredgers continued the search
certain I had gone under a log: pinned. the steady current
hounds sniffed under brush to catch my scent

miles downstream: lanterns swung out over the water
dreaming of my face. the faces I had dreamt arose
on the roads: the coats of watchers. uncloaking the new life

save those foxgloves pressed in the empty pages of genealogy
I lost the way back on purpose. the delta empties into the sea

[my lot to spin the purple: that the tabernacle should be made]

a song of Mary the mother

my lot to spin the purple: that the tabernacle should be made

with ten curtains of fine twined linen and scarlet. and the silk

and the hyacinthine. even woven with the gold and the undefiled
which is white. having the true purple for its veil

when the lot fell to me I took up my pitcher and filled it
took the purple upon my fingers and drew out the thread

in shag and floss: in coarse bottoms and in tight glossy skeins
the thrum did wind itself away from me

for a word had entered my womb and leapt inside me

I make the dark pillow where the moon lays its opaque head
I am the handmaid: pricked upon the spindle

the fine seric from the east was brought to me
soft and unfinished. dyed in the tyrian manner

of purpura and janthina the violet snail. cowrie and woodcock shell
the spiny hedgehog murex and the slender comb of venus

from betwixt my limbs arachnine the twisting issue I pulled forth

purple the night I felt the stab of the godhead in my side
purple the rot of the silk: its muscardine. its plague

a raw tuft dwindles beneath me: I feel the tug of a day ravelling
even as such gloom as this winds tight around the wooden reel

would that a potion could blot out the host inside me
grove of oak, chestnut, willow. a place of skulls. succubi

a necropolis in me rises. its colors mingle in the dark: aurora

spinster to throwster: purple my loom spread with the placenta cloth
I put a fine pattern to it: damascene sheaved and lilied

threads thrown in acute manner so that the bee rises on the border
the rose of sharon the cedar the camphire. calamus and pleasant fruits

and these even dotted with locusts caddis flies and polyphemus moths
a fountain: a garden wattled with reeds upon the weaving

garden to be betrayed in? a shadow against the breast of the tree

so the flox did luster in mine eye: in the cloth I beheld a fine water
as one might arduously with calander produce: the weft

a wave offering in my hands. pin that pierces the body

over my lap a spreading wound of purple: purple that puckers and gathers
cloaking my folds of purple. the swollen vein of a young boy's manhood

purple deep and hopeful. a scar under the frenum. a heavy prepuce

a caul. an umbilical cord. a wet sluice. an angry fist. a broken vessel
a bruise. a blemish. a raincloud. a lesion. a fissure. tissue

the ends I took up and selvaged. this veil shall not fray

and vast the warp of the cloth. sea of galilee. tigris euphrates and jordan
flow not as wide as my great bounty: undulant sky above my loom

the shuttle through me: a lance in my side. a heave in my bowels
how will the temple receive my gift: scab of purple. pustule. genitalia

[and a future who? unfurls above the altar] the thread the thread the thread

[my riches I have squandered. spread with honey]

a song of the prodigal son

my riches I have squandered. spread with honey
the arval bread in my pocket and nary a farthing

lived for a spell among roaches in a rickety squat
between the alcohol detox and the catholic church

peeled my plump white bottom. a sauvignon grape
[now exsiccated: the wizened sultana makes no golden cake]

crouched in the gulleys. wiped with leaves
cooked roadkill: topped with government surplus cheese

snuck in underage at club 21 (2121 21st street, long gone)

wastrel opal-throated bird: a molting quivers along the pinion

I fear my mucus: its endless volume and amorphous shape
a demon expelling from my lips. the moon wags its tongue

each dull morning the mirror imagines me a future: older
misshapen forest: stinging adder and sprawling spider

the way to haven seems interminable. I creak and shuffle
listen, you wilderness: make plain and let me pass

[the ice hadn't cracked. stingy ground: frozen with its hoard of bulbs]

a song of the resurrection

the ice hadn't cracked. stingy ground: frozen with its hoard of bulbs
how long would march flail us. bastinado of wind and hail

one morning I rose. declared an end to winter [though cold persisted]
convinced that the dogwood wore its quatrefoil splints of convalescence

because the land gives back. I wanted warmth within its chilled pellicle
radiating blades of *cordgrass* and *wild rye*. the demure *false boneset*

on the phone with mary my friend: she too persuaded of the thaw
so long withdrawn a blindness had us. desensitized to sneaping frost

we set out for the bluffs. surely clover pullulated along the crest
and the air   [no longer chiding]   would teem with monarchs

I had word of a marigold patch: the welkin dotted with butterflies
orange blaze: the deceit of wings and the breeze's pulmonary gasps

the journey stretched. why hurry?   the promise of the garden enough
the road a pleasant shifting through riparian forest: a windlass a wander

already I have taken a long time to tell you nothing. nothing awaited us
nothing sprouted out of the ground and nothing flew about the bluffs

brown twigs: a previous splendor born to another season. now swealing
the wick had held its brief flame: sodden. the earth received it

whitetails foraged what was left of vegetation: we startled them grazing
one cardinal held watch at the empty beds: injury in the stark white trees

in the town a church kept bare its cross: draped with the purple tunic
we knelt to the wood. and this I tell you as gospel: the sky shuddered

a bolt shook our hearts on the horizon. for what seemed an eternity
[for we knew eternity by the silence it brings]   void: then scudding rain

[when he comes he is neither
sun nor shade: a china doll]

a second song of John the Divine, as at the end

when he comes he is neither sun nor shade: a china doll
a perfect orb. when he comes he speaks upon the sea

when he speaks his voice is an island to rest upon. he sings
[he sings like france joli: *come to me, and I will comfort you.* when he comes]

when he comes I receive him in my apartment: messy, yes
but he blinds himself for my sake [no, he would trip, wouldn't he?]

he blinds *me* for *his* sake. yes, this actually happens
so that the world with its coins with its poodles does not startle

I am not special: have lied stolen fought. have been unkind
when I await him in the dark I'm not without lascivious thoughts

and yet he comes to me in dreams: "I would not let you marry."
he says: "for I did love you so and kept you for my own."

his exhalation is a little sour. his clothes a bit dingy
he is not golden and robed in light and he smells a bit

but he comes. and the furnace grows dim. the devil and the neighbors
and traffic along market street: all go silent. the disease

and all he has given me he takes back. laying his sturdy bones
on top of me: a cloak an ache a thief in the night. he comes

HEATHER RAMSDELL

ARTIST'S STATEMENT

A core sample of aesthetic strata

Why do I write? Why *do* I write? Why do any of us write or make art? Why not make something practical instead like a chair or some money? Why not make something edible that disappears and, if bad, can be easily forgotten, or if good, can live on in memory screened from damaging changes of context? *The question is: How does one hold an apple / who likes apples?* Is the question about intentionality? Is the answer to such a question to be trusted? Would it be better to continue speculating? By *better* are we talking about being more interesting or more productive? Should this answer be a record of something that has already happened, or should it be prescriptive and affect poems that have yet to be written? Can there be an experiment without a hypothesis? Is language poetry scientific? Is lyric spiritual? If a poem was written in the tradition of the avant-garde but is then absorbed by the mainstream, what is it? Is a poem less valuable if it appeals to a large audience? Can a poem be committed to the lyric tradition, even if the poet is not? Is lyric committed to beauty? Is there such a thing as beauty? Where does it reside? I mean, does it belong solely to the beholder, or does it exist on its own? How much of this has to do with writing and how much with reading? What is the correlation between value and poetry? What is the value of a gift? What is the value of meaning? Are poor poets better (poets) than rich poets? How much will my statement about writing change my poems? Are answers better than questions? By *better* are we talking about appropriateness or information? What are some distinguishing characteristics of a bad answer? How about a bad poem? Does good poetry more resemble good painting or bad poetry? Is there such a thing as beauty that exists separately from the self? Is lyric the voice of that self? When the notion of self is decentered, what happens to the actual person? Where does that person go? What exactly am I endeavoring to accomplish, or what approximately am I endeavoring to accomplish when I write poems? Or should I call them something else to escape from the prejudices against poetry that exist even in communities that care most about this kind of writing? Is accomplishment even appropriate here? If I understood my intention would I still feel the need to write? Are questions better than answers now? How about now? Maybe something doesn't need to be phrased as a question in order to be one. Maybe it can just express or, better yet, create a condition of wonder.

House Face

Containing little or nothing.
Containing five pages of paper.
And made less human, I.

A chair will be waiting.

A pink door in a black hall
hung, a tongue in her
mouth made less open.

Sounds it sung. Streaks.

Any attempt to run, punished.

To run punished in
falling repeatedly over
a chair a hair a char hail

containing similarity,
almost a figment. I—
I error.

Her in the heart.

In Spite of How

the floor the wall the wall meet

in spite of how the floor

tilts the individual point

agrees a corner is

fortunate a knob a hand is

incomplete a foot perhaps

no through the door perhaps the individual

has not a knob a hand perhaps a corner

opens no a circle is

abstract a circle cannot find its

find its ambition perhaps but thank you

perhaps a hand falls open no

but thank you through the door

in spite of the door

Where Things of a Kind

In pause, in
decent pause with plausible
care, to push the matter aside

where were we, intentional
streak on glass, we were aware

of our own breathing, meaning
flows from it, uncomfortable

laughter finds a spare
seat in the aisle, the structure,
seen from above, a grid
we cannot stand outside, allows, as

long as the axes hold true, not blow around,
as long as winds don't come, and
we are meant, not error bending, though a bent

hair on a white
tile is also true, because

isn't the idea
to have it
lifelike. Just the other day I

lost my place.
From here on let's leave crumbs, let us
feel free to walk around.

There are fields.
That line looks like a bridge.
A barge a ground, is
that a fire to your left, the trees
stop, bear with us, that
rock is that
hard, there is no need for proof

now, do not
move. Do not anything.

Bright Receding

With speed the prior body
of the tree could not have foreseen

in orange flakes rising from safety
of, this its release from,
the locus of fire into mossy night,

an imaginary fire in actual night.
Amongst blacknesses, that star already
imploded now is the size of

a rose window, actually
I made that fact up. The sun
came through the window again

by such light, some
burnt trees—such
trees in the yard make sense

having incongruities which
occlude both, dread numbs
both—both
include part-answers.
And no research gels.

In being numbers, the shadow faces
turn, locate
one end first, one part, color

of orange and red and black, black
as the black of an eye, please
find me my coat, it says.

It says, you cannot prefer both
the image and itself, you cannot reside
in the possible, henceforth,
resolving to climb inside the solid mound, not see.

If It Is True What Is Said of the Work

we'll never see the result. Refraction
through a medium other than—music
stands subsequent, a sprained surface of actions
of the inner landscape exemplified
by a stick. The stick looks bent. The stick
put through a series of tests, is tossed
striking resemblance, but a ruler must not

keep changing scale, the philosophers needn't be nice.
Later they send an invitation after preventing,
according to logic, attendance. You may never arrive
at a place but cannot remain. Nor is the expedient
replacement flagable. Pack.

They'll carry us out by the collar. The struggle
reluctant to fall wholly to either side.
No reason to mention
neurology, the terms are a stick,
its workings divided with model-makers' skill into
manageable disks, grids placed over the heap.

The table is weighed or the argument table is made of it,
an as-of-yet unbroken version of a crack compared
to an as-of-yet unbroken finger a fist, to a hammer, the table
pinned down with broad duplicity and error, an acute
pinch and incomplete
set of tools to fix the constellation, the moist
eye, the stick, a stick and a stone.

Good Sheep

A sheep running downhill makes the bell jingle faster with seeming intentionality in recognition or as doleful music of domestication, she records it. The sheep disappears beyond the crest of a small hill. She hears the bell and erases. The bell dings as the sheep walks around in the dark.

Sheep do not have the attribute of intentionality regarding bells and can mean nothing by them though an itch can cover the hunger always moving the sheep from one area of the fenced-in hill to a grassier one. The hunger is always there.

And she is always there, sensing this more and less as she moves in relation to a strand of details, violences, seeing. Bells approach and stretch away unsteadily. The bell rests somewhere strong enough to hold it. Sure to find it there when she comes back again, she turns away.

Under her kitchen table in New York a green pea is.

Over the mountains clouds flame into farther clouds with some pink leading to vastness while colors can still be detected, pinkish gray and bluish gray, in a range that gets smaller, dissolving into smoke. She closes her eyes into night which the man at the plastic bench watches carefully descending without moving.

Mountains. Without meaning something pointed the man leaves the dinner table. He goes outside to sit on a plastic bench and doesn't move.

The bell jingles, otherwise the sheep is lost. To the elements, wolves, itself, for example, left alone the sheep will freeze if the weather is cold enough, and if grass is not available will starve, and if wolves

The wolves from this region are dead.

And the angels descend upon them, and with no place strong enough to hold them go away again. She records this fact.

Against the mountains certain crying receding against less meaning.

The chair is uncomfortable, has a scratchy seat. She feels hungry. Moves, sits on the bed, lies down. She smokes and puts it out in a cup. The bed lamp smokes.

selections from "Vague Swimmers"

Now place your hand on her back. Now struggle and shove him off. Please place flowers in this problem. Now hang up on her. You enjoy the e-mail function. Please match the following pages with money. Survey the crowd applying for more money. Make at least twice as much sense. Create two small cuts, each a quarter inch in length, so we can slide in secret money. Meet me for breakfast. (See *Healthy Quick Cook*.)

Several uncomfortable minutes later, he (shirt) and she (pants) emerge bearing flowers. Place the flowers into four decorated egg cups. Okay egg cups. Okay flowers and draw money in through the slots.

Yes, I would like to have the classics brought into my home, definitely check this box.

Please bring money for this (your name appears real big in this section). Flowers are appropriate for this. Tuesdays and Thursdays are good for this.

...   .

New flaws. Food rotting within a safe context. First the food, then a flood in a sequence that is graspable and therefore comforting to us. Tucking Mr. Triangle into the blue field, contingency replaces some personal debt. Because the replacing phase should start by then as the mourning process courses through its phases. This plays out in the ideologies of other islands.

And if the problem should spread wide enough to engulf us and I show up in time to put an end to expectation, if they let me explain it as clearly as possible, plowing a fine path to future ills, not to emerge from the cube in the form of a star, probably not to emerge from the field of cubes ever, ranked according to importance, urgency, lateness, and scale, including rhetorical burlesques and the many degrees of sincerity, so that some listeners get certain parts of the point if nobody gets the whole thing, I will organize the questions into three big stacks, adding and erasing question marks as needed. In this way the miraculous peels off and can be stuck to other things.

I am very enthusiastic about this pile of rubble.

Waiting in a waiting room. Swirls on a buff-colored rug.

...   .

In repetition, minor violences grew more blunt and less precise. A violent act *about* something? This is a clock. This is a line. I'm trying not to touch the people near me with my bag, to make the experience less annoying for them avoiding touching them in ways they were unpleasantly expecting to be touched. I am trying to make myself an example of moving in crowded places, to disappear completely into the motion of getting a ticket, shedding the person to become waiting to move toward the ticket. I am hoping to improve the overall environment in this noninvasive way, standing in front of a large audience saying nothing, asking them if I am making any sense, and the good news is pointing for those who feel the words are meant to shut them out.

The subject of sorrow, she began. It started raining. Big drops from which smaller drops escaped up when it hit, five or six making the pavement unsuitable for chalk. Pedestrians stepped over the outline. Parts arms legs drooled into shapelessness. Vague swimmers swam by, shyly bleeding together. None of the people cried yet. Because the heroine was crying it took away our responsibility to cry. This, the actor proudly stated, and we were embarrassed not to have known that already. That is often what mothers do because mothers do not have feelings like the rest of us. Fathers and brothers are silent. The phone rings.

...   .

This is not about her but she is an example in this. At this show of kindness the person begins to cry. Crying happens to be my favorite sound at night. Crying in the night forms a kind of pillow or muffler for joy that might be trying to get through different flaws in the night like stars—pinholes through which crying is holes in the night and the sound of crying, when there is not other sound, is holes in the muffler so the neighbors hear and feel relieved that someone's sorrow is worse than theirs.

...   .

Thank you for saying pathos instead of pathetic, keeping us the same size as before. A picture choked down to a dot that stays. In staying, suffers. In suffering is subject to brief instances of wakefulness inflicted as we go along.

Not to forget how to get back. Once here, before we move, again, but when I got the chance to say it, it was late.

Against hard effort answers slip from oblivion. Suddenly obvious falling glass before a catching gesture, close as clothes drawn tight against next breath, before the hand, now quickly dust, capable of being blown away to join the mass, the rest of the names accidentally removed during restoration.

Not to forget how to get back. Once in, to enter again as same or similar. Unscathed. Exactly as we were.

karen volkman

artist's statement

I find myself increasingly reluctant to make definitive statements of my poetics, since the direction of my work keeps shifting and leaving me puzzling after it. One constant is certainly a preoccupation with form and formal devices as prods to intuitive engagements. For my second book, *Spar*, I started working with prose poems partly as a reaction to the use of line lengths and stanza shapes as formal devices in my first collection. I was curious to see what would happen if I did *not* have those resources for shaping the poem—what would make the piece a poem at all (according to my own particular sense of that word). This became a prolonged obsession with seeing what shapes these blocks could take based on inner tensions, musicality, fragmentation, syntactic swervings. Prose poems are fascinating in part because they tease our standard readerly expectations, startling us with unexpected movements that throw emphasis on the sentence or phrase, giving them a renewed presence and weight.

Tension, both within and between poems, is a term I value. Within my books, I imagine the poems tensed against each other, offering oppositions of tone and movement, with the reader re-positioned or asked to adopt a different stance from poem to poem. I wanted to give a sense of a movement of mind from poem to poem, a range of articulations and engagements being played out and tested.

The question of a lyric speaker is one that continues to evolve for me: in *Spar* the speaker exists only in a kind of amorous relationship to words, in relinquishing at least partly the role of creator to become a created and stranger self. This is a submission to the unknown, including an unknown otherness of our own possible selves. In my new sonnets, I've tried to suppress the "I" as much as possible, investing the poems' urgency in the dense texture of recurrent sound and imagistic collision.

An angry little machine, the sonnet. It seems an ideal form for exploring slippages of meaning and complexities of relational systems; in its orientation toward argument, it is immediately a figure for the conflicted mind. The resolute character of its syntax and the solidity and decisiveness of its rhyme scheme embody a passionate movement toward a certainty that its conflicted stance questions and resists—in this, it strikes me as a form of anguish, longing for, but never fully believing in, the solace of its own intelligent system. Some of the broad questions I am considering in these poems: What is the relationship of a musical structure to other systems—natural, divine, physiological? How do forms of intelligence interrelate? How is constraint a base for intuitive leaping, a mode of freedom? How is the poem a kind of thinking body? I believe one of the jobs of poetry is to discover and enable different and more complex ways of engaging experience, including the experience of our inner lives, partly by surprising us into developing new modes of response in reading, new freedoms. I see pleasure and intense sensation and a shock of strangeness as essential to that experience.

Untitled

Shrewd star, who crudes our naming: you should be flame. Should be
everyone's makeshift measure, rife with tending—constellations called
Scatter or *Spent Memory* or *Crown of Yes* or *Three Maids Slow in Pleasure*.
Some days my eyes are green like verdigris, or green like verdant ardor, or
like impair. Does it matter the law is a frame to hang your heart in? This
was. I saw it, schemed it, bled it. I was *then*. Or: I ran with all my leagues
of forgotten steps to reach you. A rose said to a rumor, is fame what
blooms with flanged petals, or is that cause? Are blind bones brighter in
skulled winter or spring-a-dazing? I am asking the most edgeless
questions, so words will keep them, so the green gods in my mind will lull
and lie. But constellation *Mute Cyclops*, my ravaged child, weeps every eye.

Untitled

Lady of the lake, what does all our weeping lead to? A pair of keys, paucity of summer—just because. I tasted his tears, they were salty, like a seawind—that should have been enough to set sail, acres of stray. Acres of wind-swept granary, what then? Everything blind begins in the darkness. It portends the deliberateness of an unsinking sun, past forgetting, or finishing, the room phrased, phased, like tiny nets of caught. A tree never asked for its stature. So with me. A pearl never counted its pallor as less or more. Why should winds take the pulse of *farther*, slipped along the digits of simple go, of been? No one has thoughts as pale as these—till they bleed them. I doubt more the less I grow, I taste the dark cognition, it is everybody's random. Be your own heart's ending, in the abandonment of seeming—weeping like a two-bit sermon—mistress Sum.

Untitled

Although the paths lead into the forest, we are bitter with the bodies of days that end too early. All things tend to a darker dissolution. In a pond, the green flecks adrift, the ducks are dimming, murk preserving rust brine and the fish with a marl fin. We may be guided by grieved grass, the workless, mossy flesh, which tufts the dumb stones in their staunch sleep, awake.

Women who tend the brown days can only listen, it is this that quivers—the no-time, the nothing—which birds have swallowed like lucid beads of sight. If you dig in the earth with your fingers, with your stick, what to do with the blameless accruings? You strike lack. You slap the long oblivion of a blank alive with harm. If it is morning, why are we dying? There used to be so many stories we could sing, the tongue of luck, the dreamwork. And how the days fall like random raindrops, and leave no stain, beside the quiet streams where time is seeping, bone, blame.

Untitled

I never wish to sing again as I used to, when two new eyes could always stain the sea, of tangent worlds, indolent as callows, and the clock went backward for a skip, to rise, to set.

Some will twine grass to fit in a thimble, some will carve bread to mend a craggy wall, some in the slantest midnight cry for sleep. When the pitch-owl swallows the moon, what welt will show it? Sighing helps nothing, raspberries raw and green, in the form of a heart

imperfectly divided. A wave grows sharper close to the shore. Some own words like strips of scape and summon. It is possible to suffer even in the sun. And race the steep noon to its highest, hoary gate. Stares drop under the sky; silence of a windslap; and a scar drifts out of air to stand whistling:

She who listens poorly will always be calling. She who sounds silence drowns with the dumb.

She who cuts her hands off must drink with her tongue.

Untitled

No noise subtracts it. It won't leave, or scatter jokes or fathoms, no tiny
failing, or some short multitude impossibly, or now, it would certainly
never scribble stanched fragments on this less. Noise is not, so words
think, a complex logic, no one loses reason fast enough, or then. To
murder sound, you must bleed the pastures, the so few animals and
vapors, misread the minerals, or still the static the huge stones break
when we close at night. You must never dream clouds in coils, convulsive
weathers, or those greetings we never felt leaving: nights of adulthood
whose boredom is forever explored

A sorrow not meant for anyone, an ancient beneficence ending so
softly, with such shallow and plain sustainings—days in the lavish spaces,
and nights in the desert, deserts, someone else—or is it too much to never
sleep enough, to dream? There must be forebodings of a few dawns of
contempt, none the same as any other, premonitions of a few men
whispering from pleasure, or of loud leaping boys who have never touched
death, and are opening this first time.

Untitled

I believe there is a song that is stranger than wind, that sips the scald from the telling, toss, toss. In the room I move in, a wrecked boy listened to each sky's erasing, for it was shrill winter, for it was blast and blur. For it was farther from the native birds and the gray heath heather and the uncaressable thighs of the one who shook in violet. Those who fly farthest must always burn the nest. But the mind in its implacable spectrum dims to brown. Must you die on your back like a cheap engine, rust and wrack? In the crevicing days, there are no words for prizing, between the lidless moon and the silver hands of the fountain. But if it is space you must fail in, teach it din.

Untitled

We did things more dulcet, more marionette. There were equivocations—usual modems—all sorts of agos. Then—in time—the needed accretion.

How much like a star we were, light as blazons. Nomad of a thousand paths, surely there are tempers more like yours, acrid and fulsome, whose articulated measure is a queenly Entire. Then we counted our fingerprinted petals—kept dryer in a pale tin—rose and carnation—loved, attended, tamed.

Be attention, dear border, you wander too far. Your music is dissonant sometimes, calamitous fugues and fallow, echoed tones, you are turning too many melodies into maunder. It seems we are creature, we devour and leave. But when late light turns the leaves gold, when the red pine offers its armfuls of snow, we are not hunger and perjure. In that moment (blemish and blossom) we are *gaze*.

Sonnet

As the dream a consciousness adored
beached its semblance in a mist, a mere
oval emulates a circle, austere
lack, swart spiral. Opacities are poured

in midnight ciphers, alembic of the shored
remnant, *naufrage* the hours cannot steer
north of founder, and ruin is the clear
attar on the tongue, trajectory of toward

blue as blindness in the ocean's stare.
Oh the minus when it runed and roared.
Lucid cumulus (the wind's white hair)

indignant plural of the single word,
rages, retrogrades. Omega air
all formless fire, a body of the lord.

Sonnet

A premise, a solace—deciduous dress.
A figment garment, ornament of leaves
that tip and trill and flail, kinetic sleeves
and skirt of scatter, skirting autumn's Less.

Pale-slow, slow-pale. Console the maiden, bless
her fraying figure, attenuating eves
and pale slow days when a sapped sun grays and grieves
and moon's pale plummet plurals, passionless.

Arboreal time. Bone time. Marrow grows
and, wakeful, wakes its ages, and decrees
blinding doctrines, darking—fragmented snows

seeping to sources, as a bright eye will close
in a night room, sightless. Lovers turn to trees,
trees to lovers. And each gown shreds and glows.

Sonnet

The sky we bear on our shoulders, heaven-height
and livid firmament, delineated dream
sounding distance, when distance spaces seem
silence, absence, unconsummated sight.

Atlas-Argus. Hard burden, dim delight
to bear, to blur, to peer, to stitch the scheme
opposing wind to figure, bright supreme
mind colluding in all that nascent night.

Lidded Argus, bent Atlas—caught between
world-scar, mind-ire, exigencies that blind
and hobble-harrow, double-dwindle, delete

heaven-quotient, exceeding heaven's mean.
The pain divisions. And x, the coldest mind,
skies the sentence, articulate, complete.

Sonnet

Tilt the placeless waver of this moving
over the wanton waters—spiral storm
hates the harmonies the days conform,
orage orgueil, an intenser proving

lashing its vassals, a form of loving.
Dolor, choler, how the moods deform
this ruse of light red rudiments perform—
horse and horse, fox fox, fast flick and fauving,

emblems in their leap and scrap, the livid nerving
worlds consume, design, and name a grieving.
Your impenitent animal: sky-pelt,

net and gnaw, and claw and fleet and swerving;
day's raw quiddities that roar a leaving;
eye-gold arrows, pierce-pulse; a failing felt.

Sonnet

What is this witness, the watching ages,
yield of hours, blurred nights, the blue commerce
limned limpidities the skies rehearse
dreaming their seasons, raptured in their rages.

Eventless auction the sun screams and stages
for outered spectacles that bloom their source,
or eyes are mouths and utter tongued remorse—
read me, augur, from the wrists of sages

the shocks and tangencies strangled in their veins.
Or stars are livid links in lucent chains.
Heart will read its figure in its willing

or blinded needle the compass stains;
lidless volumes and vortices of pains
distinct the dolor, and kind the killing.

Sonnet

Brown is the flat gestation of a maze
grass-grown remembrance of a second look
the field holds open like a nascent book
in which the wind has written, Sudden strays,

sudden numbers beat—the roots of days
branched intangibles a stupor took
and slept and stroked and scattered in a shook
haze of wakenings, refracting rays

outleaping their seasons, daughters of a glance
ago-ahead, a retrograde advance.
Loving nothing but the fractal ways,

they gather flowers—pearl-petal, bitter blaze—
brilliant sisters in the infinite dance
at ardor's axis, integral of chance.

Sonnet

This ellipse, slip between seasons,
a concatenation of leaves
twisting themselves in shrill sheaves
of shrivel, the rust-gray reasons

for teardrops scoring their lesions
in every substance that grieves—
and the dreaming sleeper believes,
mistress of palest collisions,

she masters the tender elisions
of eye and why and night—and bliss
(overblooming its cause) will whirl

the spring-and-autumn integral
and wide the green dying that is
black blood of whitest precisions.

Sonnet

Nothing was ever what it claimed to be,
the earth, blue egg, in its seeping shell
dispensing damage like a hollow hell
inchling weeping for a minor sea

ticking its tidelets, x and y and z.
The blue beneficence we call and spell
and call blue heaven, the whiteblue well
of constant waters, deepening a thee,

a thou and who, touching every what—
and in the or, a shudder in the cut—
and that you are, blue mirror, only stare

bluest blankness, whether in the where,
sheen that bleeds blue beauty we are taught
drowns and booms and vowels. I will not.

Sonnet

Lease of my leaving, heartfelt lack, what does
your plunge propose, your too-loose turning?
A deepfall trill, always-again returning
when Leaving, stepchild of Staying, is and was

always already going, condition, cause
of future's rapture—the baby always burning—
and present never present, always yearning
for plummet's pivot—articulate pause.

Lack lurks, blue and black. What acrid, airy sea
will give the whither anchor, heed the calling
for harbor, shore, to stall the listing lee

of always-motion, infant and appalling?
My infinite late, dark nascence: Tell me,
will there be an end to all this falling?

Sonnet

Never got, and never thought, and yet
always potent in the never-been
the ever-urge to always arc, to spin
aim's injunction in a raw roulette

ever placing never's bankrupt bet,
carbon numbers, impossible to win
at null, at zero, an integral skin:
cardinal animal in an ordinal net.

What fury frauds the nod, what squalid set?
Base Ire, base Err, base *Bas*, the baseless bane
of never's radical, the swelling square

of pallid possibles that slip and stare;
unsummed digits, unformulated stain
ever's ardor will never not beget.

Sonnet

Lifting whither, cycle of the sift
annuls the future, zero that you zoom
beautiful suitor of the lucent room
evacuating auras, stratal shift

leaping in its alabaster rift—
Lend the daylight crescent, circle, spume,
ether from your eye, appalled perfume,
ash incense to boundary when you drift

bluely looming—motion will be mute
season spooling its argent errant thread
endless loop and lavish as the dead

note resounding a transparent flute.
Tell the boys we're leaving,—wind as red
event left at the altar—the bride is fled.

Sonnet

Now you nerve. Flurred, avid as the raw
worm in the bird's throat. It weirds the song.
The *day die darkly* in the ear all wrong—
all wreck, all riot—the maiden spins the straw,

the forest falters. Night is what she saw,
in opaque increments deafening the tongue.
Sleep bird, sleep body that the silence strung,
myrrh-moon, bright maudlin, weeping as you draw

white tears, pearl iris in a net of eyes.
The spinning maiden darkens her design.
Gold gut spooling, integument of awe,

a baby breathing as a bird is wise
(the bird-bright heart that flutters like a law)
which eats the excess. The strangle in the shine.

Lawrence L. WHITE

ARTIST'S STATEMENT

If he had watched television and read no books, this could be Swinburne's poetry—that is, if he also had been raised in suburban California. Swinburne, of course, did not come to these poems directly, but rather through Pound, the first poet my first creative writing teacher sent me to. That would be another symptom: this poet wrote poetry before he read it. Pound, for all his modernism, acts out a nineteenth-century sense of beauty, as do many of his writing readers, such as Duncan (another immediate source for my sense of the poetic).

Swinburne, though, only makes sense to me read through Pound. What reading I have done is wholly informed by the Modernist reading program, their desperate assessment of the literary. Here is yet another symptom: one is called upon, by champions and detractors, to read the Modernists as triumphal. At their worst, they demanded to be read so. I have always read them as fighting to hold back an ebb tide. Whatever the literary is, it is a declining thing. I would take my own writing as evidence. But each has a station (another sign of an obsolete sensibility, the medieval sense of pluralism), and I am at mine.

An archaic sense of lyricism—limpid verging on limp, purple at heart if not in diction, moony and a mite mad—then, provides one pole of this poetics, while the kaleidoscopic phantasmagoria flashing from the cathode ray tube (at its most fervid when commanded by remote control and cannabis), stands in at the other. The glowing fragment is my second nature. Unlike the great Modernists, as exemplified by Picasso, who could work in wholes, but chose to make parts, I have no choice. I am only thankful I was not born thirty years later and medicated into shape. Nor do I feel guilty for dodging the postmodern, avant-garde draft. In the words of Pee Wee Herman, "I don't have to see it, Dotty, I lived it."

Speaking more concretely, I could say I consider *The Waste Land* as the poem of poems, or, to be more accurate, the first four sections of the poem, the anarchic choruses of distinct voices bound by some energy, some eros. Not a monument but a workshop, as Blake would have it, of the imagination, of the combinatory (a book of generation and corruption) powers that produce the human world, the poem (and any poem that strives to make a difference, to add something) makes a pledge no poet, not even the unpleasant Mr. Eliot, can keep.

Perhaps it could be left at this: if no new poems are made, all poems will be unmade. Here I put my hand to the wheel.

Emetic,

an essay on Svankmajer's Alice

Outside the theater I felt
It inside me, wanting to get out,
Like Alice in the playhouse,

And I thought this was the one time
I would see the film. The colorless screen
Flowered like smoke over the city.

Where she was sitting by the brook,
    Throwing stones into the water,
Where she was sitting in her bedroom,
    Throwing stones into the teacup,

That was putting something inside
The rabbit, investing the soul in boredom,

Of years, hours & days in the room
Of Alice staring at him inside his case, and him
Resisting her with his glass eye,
His label, *Lepus cuniculus*.

The drawer is a space inside the desk.

In the playhouse made of wooden blocks
Inside the room with the cucumber frame
With rabbit hutches inside that,

She sat at the blue pot and ladled sawdust,
Careful to pick out the screws.
                         She can't eat
Everything. Even the rabbit picked out the screws
When he ate the shavings, to fill in
Him leaking from the ventral slit.

In the drawer full of pins slithering
Each pin rings when the clasp shuts.
The ring holds
                a spark inside it.

In the drawer of pins the rabbit finds
The pain to seal his leaking cavity.

From which he pulls a watch, 5 to 12,
And hangs it on one hook
Of several screwed into the door
Hanging watches. 20 to 10.
6 past 9. 17 past 3.
                    One place over!
The hare butters the rabbit's watch.

Wait. Please sir, said Alice.
        The one time is all the time.
Sir. Please, said Alice.
        She closed each door behind her. Space

Contains more space, in the drawer of pins
Or scissors or sharpened nibs,
                            more,
Blood on the scissors, ink in the nib,

The way the body keeps whatever it eats.
Almost all of it.
                    What I remember
I get to keep, until it digests.

Next time it's my turn. Eat me, Alice.

Station. He.She.You.Me

The sycamore stretches straight,
Its new skin the color of snow,

In a file of sycamores the color of snow,
Lined against the road.

Up in the sycamore two scrannel crows
Talk, cracking the same word, seed
Of a word, slug of what matter words

Would be forged of.

                    Road.—Road.—Road.—

This road goes around the world.

    *

The headlights thrown across the street,

Pollarded sycamores draw stunted fists
Against the careless inquiry. The woman
At the payphone sees the quick headlamps

Tracing tangents, like capes, like
Oars. Free between stations,
She holds off on the cross-country
Numbers. Her fingers stir the rough
Aggregate air, which slips beneath the shrub,
Waits for thicker shadows in the spring,

    *

The stairs, flight squared against flight,
Rose. I turned. She said,
                    "What you have
Taken, take it for what I give."

    *

The park of the full moon
Of snow the color of the moon
Of light that smells like menthol, clings

Except to the trees,
Branches etched against the anodyne.

Contour lives on lines.
Inside it's empty, what daylight fills.

*

Somewhere these same stairs turn
Endlessly upward. Her words

Rise & fall, what was given
Never lost.

*

A cardinal on a fence. A black squirrel on snow.
After the thaw two crows on matted grass
Made dialogue of one repeated word.

Acanthus

Before the library, Sister Suzy
Demonstrates the fulminating green
Bush.
        —Capitals of buried columns, she says.
Remember the lecture? Stone
To word, word to herb, a figure
To wonder on.
        No I did not.

—You were seduced by sleep.
The lecture glinted in the shallows.
Professor Atmen ground himself
To dust. I spilled the bowl.

—Headstones in a weedy plot,
These figure a ruin,
An older library.
        Suzanne, I asked,
Read me a volume of the buried library.

—In this field he failed.
His dust piled the ruins,
And your sleep, a snow of ash . . .
        Here he worked
The stone against the dusk.

—Acanthus.
    She passed
The word, a debt overwrought,
Back to me. I forgot
But never will forget.

The World as I Found It

What of the night? I spent it in X,
Medieval amusement park, whose one
Attraction, the labyrinth, was built

Over an ancient city, which was itself
First pitched on landfill. I went
From my half-room at Biasin Rooms,

A scene of vegetable desolations—
My shirt stank; the hand laundry
Had not gone well—to the sinking paths.

No one lead me or followed. At this point
I heard concussion in the clouds,
And a trailing sound, like rockfall.

The night's entertainment—a sky show!—
Had begun. But would I see enough
Of it, I worried, within the canyon

Of peeling plaster, shutters haphazard
On the lath, and staining seep from
Foundation saturating the edifice,

Choking the sky view, while down the middle
A ditch full of stuff from the lagoon,
An open duct of lymph, exhibited

A cumbersome pulse? I had to make a way,
Reckoning by what light burst
Above the walls, to the island's edge.

From where the passage opened on a wallow
And concessioneers had gathered custom
By means of lamps and celestinas,

I spotted the mountain in the sky
Ignited with vascular threads of fire.
These filaments back-lit Isaiah's Portico,

Whose pediment, front-lit by firepots,
Jars of flaming creosote that soil
And illumine, displayed terra-cottas—

Venus and the crocodile, assorted vicious
Hittite seraphim and *Mater Dolorosa*.
This tableau advertised a museum

Of the natural history of thought, but busied
My view with foreground. The event unwound
Obscured, a toy cranked up at the back

Of a high shelf. So I proceeded down
The defiles, until I made the Piazza Grosso,
With its famous rock doves sleeping standing,

Mumbling their word for bread. Between the college,
Now a diaper changing station, and
The clock tower a smaller plaza adhered,

And backed into the lagoon. This was an edge,
But not what I wanted, a seat far back
And too much to the side of the stage. I could see

The act, shapeless light exploding in the soft
Heart of the mountain, to a sound effect
Created by stone wheels in a stone trough.

Back where I was, nearby the exit, noise
From the audience lagoon distracted me
With its animal indulgence, heaving

Against the pavement, setting the fretted prows
Of the beetle-dark canoes against one
Another. The whole time it did not rain,

And the vista was never found. Instead there was
A cruise ship from Odessa, tied up
On the esplanade, preposterously

High and white, an incandescent vessel,
So empty was it of passengers, who were out
Foraging their own lipid apocalypse.

At this time my shirt stopped stinging
The creases in my flesh. The cotton fused
With nerve endings, and I absorbed the air

Without resistance. Then those small stones
In my mouth, my pitted teeth, stopped squeaking.
The gearing stripped along the drive train

Of my will. I drifted to the right, off
The open space of the Via Garibaldi,
Again onto narrow paths occasionally

Blistered with a square. The stalls were closed.
The last of the night crew welled up
Under split awnings. In the sky the sound of stone

Diminished. In the ditch, at my side always,
The animal membrane slapped and sucked;
Through the patched islets the nerve-net of

The lagoon spasmodically corresponded with
An unseen moon and the wind. My path
Contracted. This was the last alley.

Across an expanded ditch a wall
Rose straight from the water, holding nothing,
No bridge or window, rose to where

The crenellation meshed with the night's teeth
And machined a featureless screen, that strained
The lightning from the clouds and atomized

The thunder. From here I turned back, this time
Following others, in their twos and threes
All spooling back to the axes of sleep.

There was one final event: My path approached
A wall, but I drew forward, for the line
Was reeling me in. A pale glow soaked

The wall like alcohol flame. Before the end,
The course transposed onto a courtyard
Awash in the same insensible burning.

It was corona to a gallery of light
The other side of the glass facade
Of a hotel lobby. Inside this tank,

In corruptionless air, two clerks suspended
At a cherrywood desk the color of a coal
Flush with heat, but clean of ash,

Attended their books. Behind them the wall,
Free of detail, held this emblem
In polyurethane: BEST WESTERN.

And thus in the moldering night town, at the limit
Of the intelligible world, I discovered
That the central idea was of California.

Soundtrack

Quicker, vivid, she starts up
& pitches her drowsiness to me.
It swims on the light of forms,
From a glyph, the body
Of the eye, a gramophone needle,
Blunted, an oily bud
That sleeps ferociously: *Let's see*
That smile again. Breath-
Evacuated lungs wait for time
To disenchant the remembered scene.
Seams never join, toothed contours
Of the trees dark on the hill
Trailing the sunset, taste of salt
As if tin fillings wept. Quicker
Than her sleep, rolling up
The constellation into a knot,
Featured fine & small, it moves
Over my heart. This happened
Last Wednesday, trees spread
Into shadow, climbing the sky
To join the night.
                    What is it?
A lot of little water, then you
Put it all together, air bubble
Caught on needles, as in
The diver's hair. The light
Is dead. What was coal
Is now a stone.

sam WITT

artist's statement

The Poetics of Fear

Although my poetics is a principle of movement and transformation, it necessarily begins in fear. It's more of a theology than a theory, really, more than just something I carry around in my head. It doesn't, in fact, actually fit inside my head, because it's much more a thing of the body than of the head. Increasingly, it has become the rough model for the way I live my life, conduct my affairs, the guiding intuition and principle by which I interact with strangers, the people I know, and the people I love (who always manage to be both). It is also the way I try to write my poems. And it starts with fear, because fear is the beginning of authenticity, or at least its most faithful herald.

I often don't know why I am afraid, but very seldom do I question it. In a similar way, it is awfully difficult to convince yourself that you believe in something that you really don't. I don't think you can have a poetry without a healthy dose of both. We have no choice to give ourselves to the flow of time, and yet often, we stubbornly resist it. Sometimes I think the entire structure of our beautiful but flawed consciousness derives itself from just this struggle: to resist time, the very flow of everything. We *think* we own and manipulate and even control the physical world, the non-human, but in reality the opposite is true: we are in thrall to its matter and to its emptinesses. Its matter weighs on us and presents us with something that we are not. Its emptinesses give us shape and an endless space to move through. The remorse of consciousness consists of the fact that in being able to comprehend and occupy the separation between me and the physical world, I am owned by that separation. I am swallowed by that distance, in almost every moment. And in those moments when I am fully conscious and fully absorbed into the physical world, those very rare moments when a balance is struck (about thirty minutes in a lifetime, on average, the Russian philosopher Gurdjieff claimed), I am almost always afraid. Which is why fear in poetry is so important. It signals a moment of authenticity. It signals that you have, in fact, arrived. To quote a true visionary, Quentin Crisp, "yes you were afraid and you see that's the nice part because fear is the only emotion we know we feel." Fear is the derivation, I believe, of authenticity; and belief is the means by which it might be possible to sustain that "nice part," when the heart actually beats, and every single little thing has some kind of significance and meaning, and we are transformed into what we are most truly: animals capable of acting and thinking at once.

For the time being, this is my poetic model. And though poetry is not really about being afraid, it's certainly the place to start. It's funny how the world works. In the current moment, we find ourselves to be in ideal metaphysical and psychic conditions to write poetry. I need not elaborate. Such is the cunning of history and the remorse, the endless remorse from which I need poetry to free me.

I want poetry to save me. From what? It doesn't much matter. Take your pick. Smallpox? Boredom? Anthrax? Stolen elections? Shrewd manipulations and corporate fraud and invented energy crises? I want it to save me from the horror of the next unnecessary war, from a list of distinctly American agonies that wouldn't fit on this page. I want it to save me from anything, not the least of which is myself. I want, in short, to be alone with it, to have nothing but its rhythms to move me along, change me, make me mean it, be saved, whatever hackneyed phrase will do. I want to cry out and have the echo be poetry. Let my last thought have something to do with poetry. Let me write a line of poetry on a banana in my senility if I last that long. Let it show me the grace to be alone with another person and think of them first, let it teach me how to rid myself of myself, if only for a few lines. Let it give me strength, and courage, and above all else honesty, for these are the simplest things that make a poem. Let it change me, at all times, let it constantly change me, from an imitation of a human being into a human being; let it always be different, as true experience, by its own nature, is always different. Let it, in the end, as with a child, be the best thing about me, the thing I cannot fake.

Ikonostasis. The Sound of the
Sea Filling a Faraway Room.

A Song of Reverse Perspective

It is not necessarily a zone of understanding
I have come to this time
As a shining, empty room near the sea
Which has filled me with its own lungs,
And desolation the light breathing makes quiver

Like a black spider inside of me,
Occupying my freedom
In bronze, rippling pages against the white wall
I was in utero with.
                              Other days
The sea erased the lines as I wrote them.

I looked until the white birds were tiny over the waves,
And then I could see them.

A gold dome shone in the distance
Come from the East. And exactly,
The sea shouted to me *sotto voce*
With its missing eggs,
As like to be extinguished in those sweet waters

When the sun set
As this place into which I'd irrevocably disappeared.
The ikon in the corner containing an infant.
The light containing smoke.
A white bird had come to watch over me while I slept.

It was a crane that beat its large wings
Into a thermal, tucked its long neck under a wing
And turned, once, a circle in mid-flight.
As if its cooing, its low moaning
Had grown out of the foam

Into these inhalations of sound,
Eaten away by a white static in the surf.

A screaming bird woke me.
Or maybe it was a child, and turned seaward,
Whereof the waves fell quietly in lag-time,

I watched them fold into the white foam, you see,
Inside the silence, which has come again,

To reach through me into that crashing surf
From another place   *D'jinn d'jinn*
Into this room where I was precisely lost,
Exhausted through,
And became a passageway

Into the moment formed of sighs.
She spoke into my ear in a strange tongue
All. As. Alas. And the sound of the surf came through my throat,
White foam, and the answer was a mirror, darkened from time
Behind which the sea slept.

In the mirror, I could see the room
From all sides at once, a symptom of many eyes,
Into which a white bird, suddenly unfolded, had come
To open its enormous, invisible wings
Over me, and the sea

Having run its beaded mercuries
Through my pores,

Was listening me into being *from* the past.

The sea had a gown of human weave
That reached through my sleep with her breathing,
Exhausted its erased pages through me, exactly,
At the weight of my chest,
The scent of exotic flowers, industrial waste.

Exactly, in life, it has entered the velocity of my sighs,

To fill the room with invisible chrysanthemums
Carried in whispers on the backs of waves:
Thousands of years ago I spoke softly of the soft sound of the sea.
Of a woman's body,
To the place where she was sleeping beside me

In waves of black hair.
I did not wish to warn you against me.
Against the way the ocean decays into this sound of surf
That eats away at us, seabirds, the breeze,
Until the white birds were tiny over the waves,

And they could look through me.

The light containing smoke
Through the cut glass of the window
From which she'd taken down those heavy drapes.
Thrown into bits of shimmer, arose, awoke:
Lain in little creatures, violet and trembling orange
On the floorboards,
Transfused through the shaking in my wrist,

Rose: an arc was falling over the sea,
Collapsing into the vibrations of missing colors.

In general, a body must be displaced
In order for those colors to appear,

Must be distended with her human droplets,

O you women and men
Formed to sigh, the way the fern moves, slowly,
On the window sill, without pain, in place-of-trembling waves,
It's enough to make you think God loves the one
Coming to her from furthest away,

Whereof one cannot speak.

And streams of bare audiotape glittered and sang in the boughs:
All. As. Alas. Be kept. Silent.
Where my heart needs music to feed it.
And so my life decays into the shape of this moment,
Where I arose just now,

Into the sound of a child bawling
From across the courtyard, in a way it hurts to be apart from,
Having delivered me into this room,
Seeking to pierce these discarded moments through which
Already, my mouths full of pollen, my stomach

Bloated with spider eggs, head shaved,
Like a golden sperm, we've been fertilized and lost.

They wrap the eggs in leaves of beaten gold,
They beat the air with the sound of this dangerous surf.

Bright immensities through which I've moved,

Of all things spacious and intimate,
Into the cramped, muttering space in me,
This clarity has come to stand around a while,

To reach through me in arteries of light,
Wounded and raw, permitted to be everywhere at once,
Quivering over me, sensing my changes,
She came to touch me all over my animal gland
The size of this room,
To lift the translucent undercurtain almost audibly,
Until a white bird, calling the shining emptiness,

Is dancing again, orbs and orbs

In decaying circles over the sea.

Thermal Signatures

'There is nothing to remember but flight.' The owl's eyes spoke.
Come with me on my flight to oblivion in their stillness.

Only in darkness does the Owl of Minerva fly.
Flight, & onely: Traffic poison, human voices, human, acoustic decay.

Carrying the terror of all silenced voices at once
Through its mechanics, brutally, at a touch.

I watched those mechanical, clockwork eyelids lift and fall.
I watched its slow eyes move with mine. The huge, red, sweeping eyes,

Through the moment, then, that had 3 hearts.

One of these was consumed away with lightness
& carefully cultivated ammonias

(Give to me a mind undarkened)—Another,
In the case of my own, small ventricle

Having combined its flightlessness with a mutilated alphabet

Behind which blue tears of burning jetfuel
Were falling through an elevator shaft.

(O sunwaters of yestermorrow, where the paths of the sun being cross,
Purify me when I am reborn, reburn),

Along the bright course in escent of sight,

I flew I through a small, meaningless birth,
Undarkened toward the sorrowing waters

Below, invia, vivisected, a species of bobbing lights
The living may not face,

(To that place where he lifted a silver bowl

Filled with rose petals, & sheep's blood, to the sun,
Thus to appease the Nations of the Dead.)

I have amniosis like the tears in God's silence.

Onely through extinction does the Owl of Minerva fly.

Come with me through the old, smoking military tunes,
Tap your foot.

Onely I flew in my long, warbling thoughts,

Exhaust in my long, long hair: A fatalism of the body.

So that I could rebirth in this clumsy, child's handwriting,
Onely through extinction as from its afterlife,

Acoustically I lived.

We had a small song with the click of a camera shutter
Embedded in hearing.

Or rather of night, it blinked: Prismatic fringes/genii-flux/now.

Dark, watermarked crossing.   A wrinkle effect in the air.

The owl's eye said 'onely' say 'one' in its still light,
& the left eyelid translucent as always.

Say 'glass' which suddenly & mechanically rolled its gaze
Through to the girl

Who wore my face, &   the 3rd heart,

Was beating its wings inside my ribcage,
Having filled the room with its own, small, immense thumping,

Just at the weight of my considerable,
My human wailing, off again, on again,

Across the broadcast waters,
Until I was simply, absurdly there.

In faint, spectral murmurs, they said
'The war is on.'

Say 'swift'   Say gathering in their movement,
Each moment consumes itself right through to the heartbeat

Of the sun onely decay of the aura in motion I flew,
My face cupped in quotation marks of aphasia,
It was dreamed to me inside the sound of these wingbeats
(Coded as scream),   it feasted on my tongue.

I was speaking the incarcerated language.

Some of them wore screams, especially those
Who no longer had bodies.

Some wore, in faint spectral murmurs,
Outgrowths of the past, whose echo was stopped,

Of bending air, light, were alive in the grand flux
Of this thinking substance, (revive,)   They flew,

Who perished lightly above the waves—owl, beat,
I am sick with fear,

I could give you the sound of its wings
If I knew its wings,

Against a coarse grain of flying
The consumed light died in a pink nest,

In the earfuture, if I had a soul,
'Theatre of War,' or so they called it.

I have caught the airborne rust
In the form of black cash,

Minerva's bird flew from my mouth,
I swallowing

Into dawn, a cosmic brain lesion, of the Birdless Aorta
Such that my mouth resembled an embryo,

'There is nothing to remember but flight.'

San Francisco, September 11, 2001

Thermal Signatures

I sing a place called Newborn
As above / So below   Having discovered just now
                           Your finger that traces my blue circle
             Herein yes a circle below where I wander on my back
Below the place where a vein has been tattooed in your long neck
              I stand at circle lying on the bed
     Speaks speaks yesterdays of affliction
Through panels of ripped ultraviolet a castrated fingertip falls to me
                With a lighttap from the Otherworld
        On my muscular eye / as Below / speaks my Below-lid blinded
We have parted to a tiny absentunderchild—am I a forehead when you enter me
     & that *me* a dark band of color
       You smiled through your sleep
         NEKroom motherlaid into my deepest petals
             To beg an arterial quiver
         A warm place called Nektar
       Undertraces me in an undercircle   Circe
    You wand this below
              Where a quiver speaks
            As below / So above / As now
    Circling through me a livingless baby you carry in your mouth
    Digested into the birthpangs of where I was / amnow
And I do not wander then not even at a touch
              The sky has incrept
               Into my preborn cheeks
        With corrosive whispers *sugarliftshallbe*
I stand at a warm zero
        Of soft tissue & human cells
        That covers my blank face of noise in the hiving
You enter at one finger at one
    Liquidated through me in warm circles at silent
From my unwrinkled center O Silent One
       Yes yes its as below yes branched into arteries in my OtherNek
        To mirror the cry of the lunatic / The dancing is contagious
   A dead fly lies bellied on the sill & she felt it too
    Divested of her eggs days ago
     NEK   which overcomes death   TAR   in its 16 fingered centicluster
      She stumbled heavily buzzed against the flat glass face of the sun

275

Through my sleep
　　　Loses me sunsubtombed on my green back
　　　　　　　　At 4:32 pm of the nuclear humanflower
　　　That moves

Andrew Zawacki

Artist's Statement

Toward a poetics

In *Mise en page* I (May 1972), Roger Munier reminds us that the etymology of *experience* signals a series of provocations. Hailing from Latin, Indo-European, Greek, and Old High German, the word enfolds the notions of peril, limit, crossing, trial, and risk. More actively, *experience* points toward these tasks: to test or try, to transport or drive, to endanger, to go to the end of. To think the poem is inseparable from thinking the concept of experience, because what experience and poetry share is precisely a commitment to disturbing, exasperating, and transcending concepts. Both the poem and experience house the negativity, the difference that threatens, at every turn, to undo them: they are never at home in themselves. Instead, they remain open to the event that would open them.

*

The poem equally takes its bearing from the related idea of excess. As Jean-François Lyotard anatomizes in *Heidegger et "les juifs"* (1988), the verb *exceed* derives from a trio of Latin roots: *ex-cedere*, to pass beyond or go out; *ex-cidere* (*cadere*), to fall outside of, to be dispossessed from; and *ex-cidere* (*caedere*), to detach by cutting, to excise. The poem, however reticent or minimalist, is a mode of excess, and as such relinquishes itself to being shoved out of its proper, submits to being broken off from what it is. Inhabited by a stranger, the poem recognizes the stranger to be none other than itself.

*

The poem puts everything into question. It elicits order, beauty, and music where chaos, ugliness, and noise reign. Inversely, where harmony is tyrannical or assumed, the poem sets out to become a force of disruption, interruption, hemorrhaging. The poem is pitched against the orthodox and a priori, against habitus and inertia, ease and assurance, utility, sitting still. Yet this violence leveled by the poem, if ostensibly destructive, is always in the service of affirmation and avowal: the poem refuses to say yes to what has not survived scrutiny under the sign of no. If it comes to us as aporia, paradox, fragment and debris, no less than in formal elegance or measure or melody, it does so because it understands that a decision ensues only from what is not already settled or even decidable. That the poem does not exempt itself from this interrogation is the emblem of its authenticity. Sparing neither itself nor its author from being unremittingly considered as a problem, the poem suspects the language that is nonetheless its ground, while, in the same movement, submitting the poet to the tremor of the question. The poet, at her greatest degree of resolution, is singular plural. At her most fragile she is less than one. In any case, she receives herself from the poem, as an advent. Her charge is to wait for its call and to offer thanks. Its imperative to ask and to suspend foreclosure conceals, in the sense of sheltering and withholding, the poem's desire to decide and to give. Hence the poet's desire, too.

*

Poems are a species of communication, often possessing the character of a secret, which happens outside the operations of logic, practical intelligibility, and the readymade language of commerce. The poem has its own reasons, centered in awe and unknowing, and refrains from holding them up to the light of day—not because it seeks obscurity or escape, but because it would speak of what arrives on the edge of speech, and because it values intimacy too highly to betray the one it speaks for or the one to whom it speaks. A poem is meant to mean the world to the one it addresses, because it constitutes the world of the one who sends it. A poem is never at the end of itself, and it regards the other, across a distance that founds their proximity, as likewise without end. Sharing an ethics of endangerment with poet and reader alike, the poem is an act of responsibility and respect, both a gift and a manner of giving.

Ascension Provisos

Ascension Proviso 1

Not, not yet, this ever revolving speculum of abeyances and ardor
its facile, its vagrant facade, not narrowing into corridors of lease
fervor fulfils an iris without exhausting engines to further advance
edifice courting luster and lust, arisen along enamor defying ascent
fragrant so the tissue bearing tremors, coaxed by a finger, a tongue

Ascension Proviso 2

Whose crux it wore aghast without reason, where else traveling led
roulade to linger past augur and singe, runoff the spar over frames
her body did not know the difference, the lengths to which she went
one inside the arraignments of another's standing outside her shape
as among the revisions, luring some crest from the contract it keeps

Ascension Proviso 3

After convicted in the visible, breaking from as anxiously as before
swerve and cut away, these raptures force the night to stay its pulse
spurn such distance the heaving, the heat, rubbing avast of the skin
water froze out back and dazzled winter where it stuttered, stopped
darkest, she said, appropriate, cold, averse to all but the vagaries of

Ascension Proviso 4

Caught between incision and fragment, rapport of once and never
split from the sinews that centered each other in contexts nullified
propping the question ajar, storm windows shattered by certainty if
lavish one might learn to call it, except for a parallel, indigent rift
would not have exerted an answer, lashing an almost lover allows

Ascension Proviso 5

Resistance uttered but no less adhered to, washing what the revenant
coming apart at the seams of her selfhood, not ecstasy but nearly ex-
protocols to intervene, attrition eliding the sheets, the shame, and yet
bereft of the senses that burden, beguile, dare not the lenient weight
dare not restitution of whatever walls once held these halves in place

Ventriloquy

Not nails but the hammer,
having been there before and vanished,
is the house.

As bones consumed by fire
become the fire.

As a boy is a god since his face
is the face of a trickster,
and a puppet is neither himself nor another.

Since voice is an echo
already too late.

Not bones but the voice that says
Be thou bone
is the flint.

That the voice is the voice of a god
and vanished through doors.

As nails are consumed by a hammer
and a puppet who burns a house
becomes the flint and then the fire.

As an echo,
having been there before,
is consumed.

That a voice saying *Be thou bone*
is not a door,

as the face of a boy
is neither himself nor another.

Since a god,
having been there before,
is already too late.

Since the house is a trickster's house
and the bones are yours.

From the Book of Divine Consolation

as if to escape were part of what it meant to strip to nothing

    *

water studying moss on a cliff, to rewrite the slant in carpskin and
    pipeline, bottle glass warped by wind and an overdue rain

if someone skips it across

too great to call over or answer

    *

forced by flashlight and echo

    *

finished rowing downriver, upwind, evening evening out to summer
    between

bone is thicker than muscle or blood and sinks to the bottom of water

    *

wait, resist, be willing

staying the angle's erosion for two hundred years, untouched except by
    storms

paused but never stopped working

    *

since punished for desiring air

looking and having failed, though he found it himself and called it his own

reminded by another stone or object on its way down

    *

might break, but is faithful, and trusts her that much: it follows

Astrelegy

Light in the shipyards is so long in coming
the stars it once belonged to aren't there any more.

Zodiac bends in formaldehyde, where the turnpike
crosses two rivers shimmying north: Gemini

making love for the last time, zero degrees in collapse.
The twins already know about order and arc,

having learned the lesson of giving up
to lay themselves down by springrusted locks

in the bridge; backwater silt records their horoscope,
folded each night and beginning to fray at the edge:

The moon, it's written, *keeps taking the sea
from the sea, and giving it back to the sea.*

Death is not for the dying:
stars above the boathouse are playing

Cyrano to light, which remembers their names
but forgets the whiteiron scars:

this leftover light is a handful of dirt
to what finished before you were born,

and even when stars come unstuck and fall through,
it tricks us, too, into mourning.

Argument for an Elemental Aesthetic

—deficiency implies
local forecast & fruition
& the climate of a country
without which it wavers:

discretion & exposure,
say, or uncompromising
intimacy of snow

—at a prospect of spruce
wrapped in burlap & twine
these are perhaps
authentic intelligences:

propane & pressed
metal, glass-
blowing, tool-&-die

or mind to which a body
owes advent & end

—consider creekthaw & say-
brook floe, nonchalance
of shipman's eddy
laminated in ice,

sandstone ritz
scattered with salt,
low watermark of a rise:

such unconstrained gestures
of central speed, at once
centripetal, insecure,

are contours
propelled by interiors
otherwise unimposed

—not derrick
but diesel & disarray,
runaway ramp
when brakes refuse braking

are limits assumed
as instance of incompletion
not its cause:

aria blurred
to a claywash crease,
bootjack hill glisted sere,

clouds disguised
by ground that does not guess
or let them go

Ampersonata

& day not breaking but already broken

& someone holding another to privilege day

& beauty is for the living, at the perimeter, not the last

& look, so quiet we hear each other think

& a lake that fell off the edge of the eye

& clearing away the rubble, & clearing away the rubble

& days of grace, moments of anguish of course

& I don't understand, I understand

& praise without & do not look back

& call it leaving the lights off, or leaving the lake for another lake

& accommodate the feint & forfeiture, & do not look

& nothing else will trade places again

& not only waving but waving again & except

& what will never be seen, never known at the edge of the eye

& water purling in carets to cover the mirror

& memoirs of air & memoirs of

& eavesdropping on the eyelids of morning

& light & less than light—

even so,   even so

Credo

You say wind is only wind
and carries nothing nervous

in its teeth. I do not believe it.
I have seen leaves desist from moving

although the branches move,
and I believe a cyclone has secrets

the weather is ignorant of. I believe
in the violence of not knowing.

I've seen a river lose its course
and join itself again, watched it court

a stream and coax the stream
into its current, and I have seen rivers,

not unlike you, that failed to find
their way back. I believe the rapport

between water and sand, the advent
from mirror to face. I believe in rain

to cover what mourns, in hail that revives
and sleet that erodes, believe

whatever falls is a figure of rain,
and now I believe in torrents that take

everything down with them.
The sky calls it quits, or so I believe,

when air, or earth, or air has had
enough. I believe in disquiet,

the pressure it plies, believe a cloud
to govern the limits of night. I say I,

but little is left to say it, much less
mean it—and yet I do. Let there be

no mistake. I do not believe
things are reborn in fire.

I believe they're consumed by fire,
and the fire has a life of its own.

Rachel Zucker

Artist's Statement

Two Synonyms for Body: Corpse and Form

"So strange an accident has happened to us, that I cannot forbear recording it."
—Mary Shelley

I am suspect. Suspect I think too much and know too little, believe my witness though of course see slant. When imagination overtakes me (remember the wave Coleridge tried to sell us, the ocean that stood in for passion?), my body can't fail to notice and gasp for the 21% oxygen atmosphere above sea level. In this giving-notice the almost-corpse pinches fiercely at the mind's eye, the eye's horizon, and reminds that for better or worse we measure quarks and trees and galaxies in relation to human figures.

I make a shape and shadow. And with these made two boys and a cool space for them to sleep. When no one is watching I carve out pieces of the world, with my sharp body lie down on life and make a me-shaped map, human continent. I press what once looked real, a Vermeer-like landscape, through my tiniest pores, into some salty unmade mound of golem. And with everything I have seen and felt and wondered attempt to render likeness. Some changeling covered in half-visible fingerprints—if I am lucky it will cry so pleadingly your milk will let down though you know I made it.

One suspect among a herd of the anthropocentric criers, I confess. With slight evidence or without proof at all I have imagined and imagine I am guilty of daily suspicions. I have looked about with awe, suspected the real world so frightening and gorgeous that I could not help but make these forms and corpses.

What I Want You to See Is She
When Not Here As in Now

the I alone, writing, wanting, the winter sun false, furious

but not   the writing   wanting   sun   only   she
in the mind without mind—as in [I want] her [to live forever] is what I want
you to see as in red riding hood on the way to the old
woman (thought *must remember*) saw [she] in her mind along
the big road men use, the mother's words making a thin
shroud around the old [she] woman—an orange tartan in summer—
still alive inside the girl no longer in the house

i. in Hebrew *bilvi* as in

little red riding hood through the woods to see the old woman said *bilv*
'I must remember, must remember the words my mother . . .' and (good girl!)
took the big road traveled by many men—

bilvi : to myself or, literally, "in my heart"

"I want you to live"——in [my heart] not for [my self]

ii. description doesn't help

I want to explain not show but it isn't
possible [you]   have only my word perhaps her photo possibly
empathy but that brings so many interlopers into   the apartment, between u
on the horse-shoe shaped beige couch—get out!—she's quiet still
alive
I want to sit a minute more her

this memory
a too hot room her under the orange tartan I sweating in floral maternity—leave

alone

iii. I wanted her to live forever.

is not an expression of

self, my anything   I wanted her to live.

iv. "if only"

but language cannot help   rope bridge to the wrong village

v. the gate was already unlocked
                    left open   philosophers have been here and poets
and all kinds of thinkers picked their way years ago around the house for family photos
      self portraits shards crockery diaries   to express self or not self
to unimagine the house it-self is no new idea

                    she death tremendous not unusual

                          so don't *use* it

                    she   to express   others are   not an expression of
my or interiority   not even the balloon or plastic bag caught up
in air currents above the buildings   is emblematic

                    my loneliness separate   from everything

vi. I would be the wolf that swallows
            the little girl brings bread and meat or soup and drink or so the story goes
the old woman (in one version a grandmother in another not) hasn't got a chance
      the old woman hasn't got soup or bread meat or drink or any chance

            in this case she stopped eating long even before death
      it was a relief not to bother the pancreatic had the upper hand she was feeding
the wrong beast still not to come *á table* was unusual not even clear broth
      bread   eventually ice chips

            the details in different versions. . .

VII. The wolf smelled her out her age itself foreshadowing and the forest

obvious   foolish girl ("must remember"), words won't

must must remember want her   to—

in the last days the tartan I can't help describe remember I was so big she always said when is it when is the baby what day do you but couldn't finish—meanwhile he was kicking and I was trying to cook him faster and push him out to see she barely made a mark along the horseshoe beige couch so thin from not even broth just ice chips a straw of water I wanted her to stay near to be forever and she stayed and she stayed and she took water through a straw, disappearing the ice chips her lips too dry to say what would she anyway until the baby in her arms last time I saw she almost just a bony cage body what we call human no longer describes and I took the baby and weak myself went away just two days I wanted her to live and live to stay not just see him but be there when I wanted her to be not emblematic not life-process but alive

months

she

only inside

the orange tartan, too hot room; it is now

November on the big road used by many men

would I were the wolf and she inside

(whole; no mind; alive)

would I could describe but have only my, I, body

wish: "I wanted her to live"

and the child and you know nothing of it
this terrible swallow I suffer I long to open show

she

here is a thin pencil

come, woodcutter

split me down the center

in the morning gone again and only body, presence but not is—is this what I married? he here, a given—is as in: situation, situated (choice made before)—

some search for the soul or mind in the body: head, heart, blood I think it is
a membrane around the void, a scrim between skin and bones—I almost feel it lingering,
clinging—it is not deep but rooted to itself—contained (not leaking) not actually touching—one cannot touch it—doctors open but do not find, open but not reveal—
the child breaks the body and does not contain—see: I am intact around avoid
inside the weather of everything—

situation: we are two within a larger—each around an empty inside a pulled skin—
sometimes in contact we have no choice but choose proximity to make a smaller system—parcel, context—block out the too bright heavy rain verdant—decadent, fetid,
fallow—what I am trying to describe is disappearance: what happened and how he can
be and invisible, be but not is—even the language knows it, fact without gerund—voice with
edges but not edgy—

sacristy

what if you only had one scene to work with, say the nativity or the annunciation
and it had to say everything and was the only story you had—the angel over and over
slightly different tiles, flat or this time perspective—it has will has the same
ending
but the curve of her hand, no thank you, slope of her gaze say something new—today
she hides behind the scene—the angel's arms crossed at the wrists like a double
bow
but also—look again—like an embrace

how dare he with his golden curls the angel presumptuous his down-turned eyes and
folded wings—he has already removed his shoes and has beautiful feet—she alone,
not yet
of child, in some grand palazzo says shyly, no thank you, her hand poised in half
prayer
position not altogether proper—open, possible—the other stubborn on the book—
not yet a virgin her blue is French almost gray

then when time flattens the big fish comes to swallow Noah ark and all and
Mary
in her blue kimono goes to Holefernes—deep deep into the center someone has
taken
her desire, her own desire and used it to fashion a child—tired of being shy—
deep
deep into the colonnade one vertebra at a time someone has taken her and left a
little
changeling in exchange her now a virgin except that in the sheer flimsy of her
negligee
a knife and map of the jugular

portrait of unknown

       a pomegranate, calais lily, sprig of rosemary, meanwhile we do not
say but rather tell
and tell around the jelly-centered heart—come away! soft sugary
evidence—what is the form
       of a woman besides body?—there were flowers a given and a garden—
one must
pay to enter but may leave as one desires—unencumbered by regret or so
they said but the story
       refuses to unfold peacefully—the past a torn ticket or smeared
receipt—the story refuses
to reveal or adhere but is dropped behind, a savory trail, birds circle
wearily—I should have
       brought pearls or marbles or pen caps—instead or *in her place an
anemone*—where I
go down springs up a delicate poison to mark descent: flower between my
lips—

cloister or "vietato toccare le rose"

the church no matter how big is the idea of space but not space—they
have painted
the windows which are sharp and pedantic, they have hung paintings in all
the alcoves
and in the paintings are windows and in the windows people look out
at pictures
of the world—they are therefore never going out and when pictured the
child pale
white and shrunken, the mother young and small in her dark blue
there is no escaping
the painting the world not real as it is allegory this place a huge tomb—
turns out there is a price
for leaving—now we have found other places small places banal to
inhabit
and it is not so easy to break a gash in the wall and look out—

outside, the cloister is: breath, sinus, the habitable—here day comes
into its own
and takes me with it—into itself a light blue with folds and tiny flaws—who
knows
if the column reaches up or down or even reaches as much as is and
is again
but this time not a cage—the roof surrounds what is not roof, the walls
create an inside-out:
cloister—a woman could breathe here, someone celibate—building
outside,
air in—a woman could live among other women exposed and enveloped—
but this is
never what I choose—a boy drawing, long sleeved thermal under a
short sleeved T,
like a fallen Mormon looks up as if through to sketch what is not there—
don't touch the roses,
don't trample the grass—it's *interdit*, *vietato*—and the past meanwhile
that shabby habit insinuates and even the light blue day can't protect
me

post card (central park)

    Jesus in the water does not look clean or fish-like or marine at all but only unafraid
as if he knew he had gills as if the oxygen in the sea was the same as air—I will not
    get clean but will drown I have one name only—a spider rests in his lazy cross of web high up above the park bench—one branch to another—why in the world did the dove's
    tiny sprig comfort Noah? he had no gills—

    I see now I was not the subject but location—the dove spies an ark on the horizon
then atop the mountain beached, harbored—and see how they occupy the pagan temples
    slap on another fresco—now who does it belong to?—the architect won't live to see it
so designs his plot inside—now these first buds some plot within my very death I hardly mind
    have eyes enough to see: this ravishing, there may not be another like it—

FurTHer ReaDInG

Bellen, Martin. *The Tales of Murasaki and Other Poems.* Los Angeles: Sun and Moon Press, 1999.

——. *The Vulnerability of Order.* Port Townsend, WA: Copper Canyon Press, 2001.

Bang, Mary Jo. *Apology for Want.* Hanover, NH: Middlebury College/University Press of New England, 1997.

Browne, Laynie. *Rebecca Letters.* Berkeley, CA: Kelsey St. Press, 1997.

Campbell, Barbara. *Erotic Distance.* Kirksville, MO: Truman State University Press, 2003.

Carr, Julie. *Mead: An Epithalamion.* Athens: University of Georgia Press, 2004.

Caton, Robin. *The Color of Dusk.* Richmond, CA: Omnidawn, 2001.

Clark, Jeff. *The Little Door Slides Back.* Los Angeles: Sun and Moon Press, 1998.

Clover, Joshua. *Madonna Anno Domini.* Baton Rouge: Louisiana State University Press, 1997.

Cully, Barbara. *The New Intimacy.* New York: Penguin Books, 1997.

Davis, Olena Kalytiak. *And Her Soul Out of Nothing.* Madison: University of Wisconsin Press, 1997.

England, Amy. *The Flute Ship "Castricum."* Dorset, VT: Tupelo Press, 2001.

——. *Victory and Her Opposites: A Guide.* Dorset, VT: Tupelo Press, 2004.

Estes, Angie. *Voice-Over.* Oberlin, OH: Oberlin College Press, 2002.

Favilla, Candice. *Cups.* Athens: University of Georgia Press, 1992.

Fishman, Lisa. *Dear, Read.* Boise, ID: Ahsahta Press, 2002.

Ford, Katie, *Deposition.* St. Paul, MN: Graywolf Press, 2002.

Gizzi, Peter. *Artificial Heart.* Providence, RI: Burning Deck, 1998.

——. *Periplum: or, I the Blaze.* Penngrove, CA: Avec Books, 1992.

——. *Some Values of Landscape and Weather.* Middletown, CT: Wesleyan University Press, 2003.

Greenfield, Richard. *A Carnage in the Lovetrees.* Berkeley: University of California Press, 2003.

Henry, Brian. *American Incident.* Cambridge, UK: Salt Publishing, 2002.

——. *Astronaut.* Pittsburgh, PA: Carnegie Mellon University Press, 2002.

——. *Graft.* Kalamazoo, MI: New Issues Press, 2003.

Kalendek, Julie. *Our Fortunes.* Providence, RI: Burning Deck, 2003.

Keelan, Claudia. *The Devotion Field.* Farmington, ME: Alice James Books, 2004.

——. *Refinery.* Cleveland, OH: Cleveland State University Poetry Center, 1994.

——. *The Secularist.* Athens: University of Georgia Press, 1997.

——. *Utopic.* Farmington, ME: Alice James Books, 2000.

Lawler, Patrick. *A Drowning Man Is Never Tall Enough.* Athens: University of Georgia Press, 1990.

——. *(reading a burning book).* Lima, OH: Basfal Books, 1994.

Liu, Timothy. *Burnt Offerings.* Port Townsend, WA: Copper Canyon Press, 1995.

——. *Hard Evidence.* Jersey City, NJ: Talisman House, 2001.

———. *Say Goodnight*. Port Townsend, WA: Copper Canyon Press, 1998.

———. *Vox Angelica*. Cambridge, MA: Alice James Books, 1992.

O'Brien, Geoffrey G. *The Guns and Flags Project*. Berkeley: University of California Press, 2002.

Paola, Suzanne. *Bardo*. Madison: University of Wisconsin Press, 1998.

———. *Glass*. Princeton, NJ: *Quarterly Review of Literature* Poetry Series, 1995.

———. *The Lives of the Saints*. Seattle: University of Washington Press, 2002.

Prufer, Kevin. *Fallen from a Chariot*. Pittsburgh, PA: Carnegie Mellon University Press, 2005.

Reynolds, Rebecca. *The Bovine Two-Step*. Kalamazoo, MI: New Issues Press, 2002.

———. *Daughter of the Hangnail*. Kalamazoo, MI: New Issues Press, 1997.

Ronk, Martha. *Desire in LA*. Athens: University of Georgia Press, 1990.

———. *Eyetrouble*. Athens: University of Georgia Press, 1998.

———. *State of Mind*. Los Angeles: Sun and Moon Press, 1995.

Scattergood, Amy. *The Grammar of Nails*. Berkeley, CA: Creative Arts Book Company, 2001.

Shaughnessy, Brenda. *Interior with Sudden Joy*. New York: Farrar, Straus, and Giroux, 1999.

Sobelman, 'Annah. *The Tulip Sacrament*. Middletown, CT: Wesleyan University Press, 1995.

Stonecipher, Donna. *The Reservoir*. Athens: University of Georgia Press, 2002.

Vaeth, Kim. *Her Yes*. Cambridge, MA: Zoland Books, 1994.

Webster, Catherine. *The Thicket Daybreak*. Fort Collins: Center for Literary Publishing/University Press of Colorado, 1997.

Williams, Tyrone. *c.c.* San Francisco: Krupskaya, 2002.

Willis, Elizabeth. *The Human Abstract*. New York: Penguin, 1995.

———. *Second Law*. New York: Avenue B, 1993.

———. *Turneresque*. Providence, RI: Burning Deck, 2003.

Wohlfeld, Valerie. *Thinking the World Visible*. New Haven, CT: Yale University Press, 1994.

Young, Brian. *The Full Night in the Street Water*. Reno: University of Nevada Press, 2003.

contributors

Dan Beachy-Quick's first book, *North True South Bright*, was published in 2003. He received his BA from the University of Denver and his MFA from the University of Iowa, and currently lives in Chicago, where he teaches in the Writing Program at the School of the Art Institute of Chicago.

Jasper Bernes grew up in Los Angeles and received his MFA from Cornell University. His poetry has been published in *Beloit Poetry Journal*, *Black Warrior Review*, *Seneca Review*, and other journals.

Cynthia Cruz received her BA in English from Mills College and her MFA at Sarah Lawrence College and currently lives in New York City. Her work has appeared in *Chelsea*, *Grand Street*, *New Orleans Review*, *Paris Review*, *Pleiades*, and other journals. She has been a finalist for several manuscript contests. Recipient of fellowships from Yaddo and the MacDowell Colony, Cruz has taught writing and literature widely in the New York City area.

Jocelyn Emerson holds degrees from Smith College (AB) and the University of Iowa (MA, MFA). She is completing an interdisciplinary PhD in Renaissance Studies at Boston University, specializing in early modern English literature and the history of science. She is also the associate director of the Honors Program at BU. Her first book, *Sea Gate*, was published in 2002.

Michele Glazer is the author of *It Is Hard to Look at What We Came to Think We'd Come to See*, which won an AWP Award and was published in 1997, and of *Aggregate of Disturbances*, which won the Iowa Poetry Prize and was published in 2004. She has also edited *Writers Collective*, an anthology of Oregon poets. Glazer earned her MFA from the University of Iowa Writers' Workshop. She has received fellowships from the National Endowment for the Arts, Oregon's Literary Arts, Inc., and the Regional Arts and Culture Council.

Matthea Harvey's books are *Pity the Bathtub Its Forced Embrace of the Human Form* (2000) and *Sad Little Breathing Machine* (2004). She received her MFA from the University of Iowa and lives in New York City.

Joan Houlihan received her MA in English from the University of Massachusetts. She is the author of *Hand-Held Executions*, a collection of poems and essays (2003), and a chapbook, *Our New and Smaller Lives*. She is editor of *Perihelion*, an online journal of contemporary poetry, reviews, translations and interviews, and author of the online column *Boston Comment*.

Christine Hume is the author of *Musca Domestica* (2000), winner of the Barnard New Women Poets Prize, and *Alaskaphrenia* (2004), winner of the Green Rose Award. The Colorado Council on the Arts, the Fine Arts Work Center in Provincetown, the Fund for Poetry, Writers at Work, and the Wurlitzer Foundation have awarded her fellowships and grants. She teaches at Eastern Michigan University.

Catherine Imbriglio received her BA from Regis College, her MAT from Boston College, and her MA in creative writing and PhD in English from Brown

University, where she directed the Writing Center for several years and is currently a lecturer in English. Her poems have appeared in *American Letters and Commentary*, *Conjunctions*, *Denver Quarterly*, *Epoch*, *New American Writing*, *Pleiades*, and other journals. She has received a fellowship from the Rhode Island Council on the Arts.

Joanna Klink received her PhD in Humanities from the Johns Hopkins University and her MFA in Poetry from the University of Iowa. Her first book, *They Are Sleeping*, was published in 2000. She is working on a second book of poems, *Circadian*, and a book on "complex" poetries called *You*, which takes as its central example the poetry of Paul Celan. She teaches in the MFA Program at the University of Montana.

Malinda Markham received her MFA from the University of Iowa and her PhD from the University of Denver. Her first book, *Ninety-Five Nights of Listening*, was published in 2002 as winner of Breadloaf's Bakeless Prize in Poetry. She lives and teaches in Tokyo, Japan.

Mark McMorris received his MFA and PhD from Brown University and currently teaches at Georgetown University. He is the author of *The Black Reeds* (1997) and *The Blaze of the Poui* (2003), as well as three chapbooks, *Palinurus Suite*, *Figures for a Hypothesis*, and *Moth-Wings*.

Jenny Mueller's poems have appeared in *Atlantic Monthly*, *Chicago Review*, *Colorado Review*, *Epoch*, *TriQuarterly*, and other journals, as well as in *The Best American Poetry 1994*. She received her MFA from the University of Iowa and teaches at McKendree College.

Laura Mullen is the author of *The Surface*, a National Poetry Series selection, *After I Was Dead*, and the postmodern Gothic novel *The Tales of Horror*. She writes fiction and criticism as well as poetry, and is a translator as well as a hypertext author. She currently teaches at Colorado State University. Her awards include Ironwood's Stanford Prize, MacDowell fellowships, a Rona Jaffe Award, and a National Endowment for the Arts fellowship.

Amy Newman's books are *Order, or Disorder*, which won the 1994 Cleveland State University Poetry Center Prize, *Camera Lyrica*, which won the 1999 Beatrice Hawley Award, and *fall*. She received her BA from SUNY Brockport and her PhD from Ohio University, and teaches at Northern Illinois University.

Geoffrey Nutter's book *A Summer Evening* was published in 2001 as winner of the Colorado Prize for Poetry. He received his BA from San Francisco State University and his MFA from the University of Iowa and currently lives with his wife and daughter in New York City.

Tracy Philpot writes that "I have published two books of poetry: *Incorrect Distances* and *Distance from Birth*. I have an MA and PhD in English Literature from the U of Denver. My husband, son, animals, and I live in Seldovia, Alaska, a small coastal community off the road system. We are off the grid and use solar power. I work as an advocate for victims of domestic violence and sexual abuse and assault."

D. A. Powell's books are *Tea* (1998), *Lunch* (2000), and *Cocktails* (2004). He received his MFA from the University of Iowa and is currently Briggs-Copeland Lecturer in Poetry at Harvard University.

Heather Ramsdell holds degrees from The Cooper Union and City College of New York. Her first book, *Lost Wax*, was published in 1998 as a National Poetry Series winner. She lives in New York City.

Karen Volkman's books of poetry are *Crash's Law*, a National Poetry Series selection, and *Spar*, which received the Iowa Poetry Prize and the 2002 James Laughlin Award from the Academy of American Poets. Recipient of awards and fellowships from the NEA, the Poetry Society of America, and the Akademie Schloss Solitude, she has taught at several universities across the country.

Lawrence L. White received his BA from the University of California at Berkeley and his MFA from the University of Iowa; he is currently completing his PhD at the University of Washington. His poems have appeared in *Boston Review, Epoch*, and elsewhere. He lives in Tacoma, Washington, with his wife and two daughters.

Sam Witt received his BA in English from the University of Virginia and his MFA in Creative Writing from the University of Iowa. His first book, *Everlasting Quail*, was published in 2001 as winner of Breadloaf's Bakeless Prize in Poetry. He has been a Fulbright Fellow in Russia. For the time being, he lives in New York City.

Andrew Zawacki is the author of two books of poetry, *By Reason of Breakings* (2002) and *Anabranch* (2004), and of a chapbook, *Masquerade* (2001), which received the 2002 Alice Fay Di Castagnola Award from the Poetry Society of America. He is coeditor of *Verse* and, as a former fellow of the Slovenian Writers' Association, edited the anthology *Afterwards: Slovenian Writing 1945–1995* (1999). A past Rhodes and Fulbright scholar, he is pursuing a PhD in the Committee on Social Thought at the University of Chicago.

Rachel Zucker was born in New York in 1971, and has degrees from Yale and the Iowa Writers' Workshop. Zucker's first full-length collection is *Eating in the Underworld* (2003). Her second collection, *The Last Clear Narrative*, will be published in 2004. Her long poem "Annunciation" was published as a limited edition chapbook. Her work has also appeared in *The Best American Poetry 2001*. She lives in New York City with her husband and two sons.

ACKNOWLEDGMENTS

All artistic statements are original to this volume and copyright 2004 by the individual authors.

Dan Beachy-Quick: "Echo & A," from *North True South Bright*, copyright 2003 by Dan Beachy-Quick. Reprinted by permission of Alice James Books. "Halt (Naïve)," from *Spell*, copyright 2004 by Dan Beachy-Quick. Reprinted by permission of Ahsahta Press. All other selections printed by permission of the author. Copyright 2004 by Dan Beachy-Quick.

Jasper Bernes: All selections printed by permission of the author. Copyright 2004 by Jasper Bernes.

Cynthia Cruz: All selections printed by permission of the author. Copyright 2004 by Cynthia Cruz.

Jocelyn Emerson: "Night Blindness," "The Lighthouse," "Architecture (II)," and "Apophatic," from *Sea Gate*, copyright 2002 by Jocelyn Emerson. Reprinted by permission of Alice James Books. All other selections printed by permission of the author. Copyright 2004 by Jocelyn Emerson.

Michele Glazer: "All That in the Voice I Have Adopted for This Lie," "'The Purpose of Design Is to Make the Whole Greater Than the Sum of Its Parts,'" and "Science," from *It Is Hard to Look at What We Came to Think We'd Come to See*, copyright 1997 by Michele Glazer. Reprinted by permission of the University of Pittsburgh Press. "2 Blinds & a Bittern," "Wherein space is constructed that matter may reside in . . . ," "Matter," "box," "Echo to Narcissus," "Sonnet," "Early Romance, Japanese Garden (*in the heart of the city*)," and "Map," from *Aggregate of Disturbances*, copyright 2004 by Michele Glazer. Reprinted by permission of the University of Iowa Press.

Matthea Harvey: "Translation," "Nude on a Horsehair Sofa by the Sea," "The Festival of Giovedo Grasso," "Thermae," "Image Cast by a Body Intercepting Light," and "One Filament against the Firmament," from *Pity the Bathtub Its Forced Embrace of the Human Form*, copyright 2000 by Matthea Harvey. Reprinted by permission of Alice James Books. "The Crowds Cheered as Gloom Galloped Away" and "Introduction to Eden," from *Sad Little Breathing Machine*, copyright 2004 by Matthea Harvey. Reprinted by permission of Graywolf Press, St. Paul, MN.

Joan Houlihan: "Biological Imperative" and "*H. Antecessor*," from *Hand-Held Executions*, copyright 2003 by Joan Houlihan. Reprinted by permission of Del Sol Press. All other selections printed by permission of the author. Copyright 2004 by Joan Houlihan.

Christine Hume: "True and Obscure Definitions of *Fly*, Domestic and Otherwise," "Lies Concerning Speed," "A Million Futures of Late," and "Miraculous Panoptic Precipitations," from *Musca Domestica*, copyright 2000 by Christine Hume. Reprinted by permission of Beacon Press. "The Truth about Northern Lights," "Night Sentence," "Arctic Sun," "Log Written by an Unknown Hand in

index